My boyfriend, Mitchell Proctor, is the most annoying male I know. At least, he used to be, before our hideous experience with my brother, Zach.

Mitchell can still be extremely irritating, but my brother is the major blight on my existence, as you will soon see.

Zach is only seven years old, so he's not a full-fledged male yet. However, when he is a full-fledged male, I am confident that he will be a contender for Man Most Likely to Get on Your Nerves, right up there with Mitchell Proctor. . . .

point

I Love You, I Hate You, Get Lost

Ellen Conford

SCHOLASTIC INC.
New York Toronto London Auckland Sydney

ISBN 0-590-45559-1

12 11 10 9 8 7 6 5 4 3 2   5 6 7 8 9/9 0/0

Printed in the U.S.A.   01

CONTENTS

I Love You, I Hate You, Get Lost

I LOVE YOU,
I HATE YOU,
GET LOST

My boyfriend, Mitchell Proctor, is the most annoying male I know. At least, he used to be, before our hideous experience with my brother, Zach.

Mitchell can still be extremely irritating, but my brother is the major blight on my existence, as you will soon see.

Zach is only seven years old, so he's not a full-fledged male yet. However, when he is a full-fledged male, I am confident that he will be a contender for Man Most Likely to Get on Your Nerves, right up there with Mitchell Proctor.

What exactly is it that makes Mitchell so annoying?

For one thing, he is a creature totally ruled by impulse and emotions. He doesn't plan, he doesn't organize, he doesn't analyze. He just *does*.

This is how I make a decision: I want to go to a movie on Saturday. I look at the movie listings in the newspaper. I read the reviews. I listen to the critics on TV. I pick the movie I want to see.

This is how Mitchell makes a decision: "I got tickets for the Tone Def concert!"

"Who is Tone Def?" I ask.

"They're a new group."

"I've never heard of them," I say.

"Me, neither," says Mitchell.

"Have they made a record?"

"I don't know," says Mitchell.

"What kind of music do they play?" I ask.

"I don't know."

"Then how do you know we'll like them?"

"How will we know if we *don't* like them," asks Mitchell, "if we don't go to their concert?"

What kind of sense does that make? Spending seventy dollars on tickets for a concert you might hate?

And he's totally irresponsible about keeping appointments. He'll show up an hour late when we're supposed to meet somewhere, with some lame excuse like how there was a fire in a paint store.

"It was incredible!" he'll say. "The flames shot up fifty feet in the air! You should have seen it."

"I couldn't see it," I'll remind him. "I was waiting *here*."

Or he'll show up an hour *early* for a date, when I'm still in the shower and no one's home, and I have to answer the door in a bathrobe with my hair dripping into my eyes.

"You're not supposed to be here yet," I'll say.

"I couldn't wait to see you," he'll say.

"Well, here I am," I'll grumble. "And I'm a mess."

"No you're not. You look cute wet."

Now, how can you scream at someone who tells you you look cute wet? It's maddening.

Or we'll be studying for a test. That is, I'll be trying to study, and Mitchell will get restless. I'm struggling to memorize Spanish vocabulary, and suddenly a carnation made out of Kleenex will land on my book.

"Mitchell! Stop it."

"Don't you like it when I send you flowers?"

Two minutes later, a paper airplane will graze my head.

"Mitchell, cut it *out*. We're supposed to be studying."

"Read what it says."

I look at the wing of the paper airplane. On it, in Mitchell's scrawl, are the letters FWAK.

"Fwak? *Fwak?* What in the world does that mean?" I ask, even though I know I should ignore him.

"Flown With A Kiss," he says.

"Mitchell," I'll scold, "this is a very important test and you are acting extremely childish."

"I can't help it," he'll say. "I'm young at heart."

"Yeah," I'll snap back, "and you've got the brain of a six-year-old."

"But the body of a Greek god," he'll joke, and put his arms around me and his lips on my hair, and not only will I forget the Spanish vocabulary I've been studying, but all the Spanish I learned in the last two years.

And then what will happen? (No, I mean after that, the next day.) He'll get a 95 on the test, and I'll get a 73.

Now you may well ask, if your boyfriend is the most annoying person in the whole world (except for your brother), why is he your boyfriend? Why don't you dump him and find a nice, soothing, reliable boy, someone responsible, sensible, predictable? Someone, in other words, more like myself.

A reasonable question. The answer is that when Mitchell is not being annoying, he's sweet and funny and loyal. And charming and old-fashioned. He's the only boy I ever met who can do the tango. And *wants* to.

By the time I found out he makes me crazy, I was already crazy about him.

What I'm going to tell you about happened on our six-month anniversary. We'd been going together since December, and we'd planned a special anniversary celebration.

He'd made reservations for a sunset dinner cruise on an old-fashioned riverboat that sailed around Long Island Sound. There would be a DJ who played big-band music, which we both love, and dancing. ("Maybe he'll even play tangos," Mitchell speculated.) It was supposed to be very romantic.

I'd been looking forward to it for weeks. I had a new dress that was almost elegant — perfect for dancing — and I found myself humming "Ol' Man River" wherever I went.

And then, four hours before the cruise, disaster struck.

I was soaking in a bubble bath when my

mother knocked on the bathroom door. "Dana? Aunt Sarah's getting married!"

"That's wonderful," I said. My aunt had been divorced for seven years. "When?"

"Tonight."

"*Tonight?* Are you kidding?"

"I'm not kidding." There was a desperate edge to her voice.

"To whom?" I asked.

"Some guy she's only been seeing for a few weeks," my mother said. "It's crazy."

"Yeah, maybe." I wiggled my toes in the bubbles. "But it's great, too."

"I don't think you're going to feel that way when I tell you what I have to tell you."

"What do you have to tell me?"

She told me.

"I'm going to drown myself!" I shrieked. "Don't try and stop me. The door's locked!"

"I'm sorry, I really am," she said. "But we just couldn't find anyone to stay with him, and we can't take him with us to Maryland. After five hours in a car, he'll be a monster at the ceremony."

"Oh, no, you can't take Zach to Maryland, but I can take him on a three-hour romantic dinner cruise and spend my whole romantic anniversary chasing him around a boat and digging mashed potatoes out of his ears. Goodbye. I'm drowning myself now. Tell Mitchell I'm sorry to break our date."

I slid halfway down into the tub until my chin sprouted a puffy beard of bubbles. "Glub glub!" I said loudly. "Gurgle."

"Dana, I'm sorry, but it can't be helped. And we have to leave in an hour. Please don't drown yourself."

"Why not?" I demanded. "I have no reason to live."

"Well, for one thing," she said, "the police will come and have to break down the bathroom door and they'll find you naked in the tub and it'll be very embarrassing for everyone."

"Wait a minute!" I sat up. "You need reservations for the cruise. We only have reservations for two people. We can't possibly — "

"I called the ticket agent. They weren't full." A long pause. "You have reservations for three now."

"That's it!" I screamed. "I'm going under for the third time!"

But, as you have figured out by now, I didn't drown myself. Although I was tempted to lure Zach into the bathroom and drown *him*.

Instead I dried myself off, phoned Mitchell,

and offered to postpone our anniversary cruise.

"But then it won't be on our anniversary," he said. "Let's go anyway. Zach and I get along pretty well."

"I don't want to spend the evening watching you and Zach get along," I said.

"Look, Dana," he said quietly, "if it's a choice between being with you and your brother, or not being with you at all, I choose you and your brother."

I nearly cried. "Oh, Mitchell, that sounds so *mature*."

"Yeah," he said. "I always sound mature when I'm depressed."

If Mitchell was depressed, he certainly didn't act it when he came to pick us up. "Hey, Zach, you look spiffy."

Zach was wearing his only dress-up clothes — a navy blazer, gray pants, white shirt, and a novelty bow tie in the shape of a vampire bat.

"Yeah," he said sullenly. "Dana made me."

It had taken me longer to get him dressed than it had taken to get me dressed. Mainly because I had to spend an hour threatening to set fire to all his other clothes if he didn't wear these.

He'd slicked back his dark hair with gel so it was plastered to his skull. His head looked like a wet bowling ball.

"And you," said Mitchell, taking my hand, "are beautiful."

"I thought you'd never notice." I leaned my head against his cheek.

Zach made gagging noises.

It was a half-hour drive to the pier where the *Queen of the Bay* was docked. Zach spent most of the ride asking if we were there yet, and was there a bathroom on the boat?

I spent most of the ride planning in which order I would murder my relatives.

We parked in a lot right next to the pier. There was a line of people at the gangplank waiting to board. The boat was an old-fashioned paddle wheeler, all painted white, with fancy railings and two decks. Dixieland jazz filled the air as we joined the line.

"Isn't it beautiful!" I said. "It looks just like the one in *Showboat*."

Mitchell nodded happily. "It's great," he agreed. "Like a trip back in time."

"I have to go to the bathroom," Zach said.

Mitchell got us to the front of the line by explaining Zach's urgent need to the ticket taker. They checked off our reservations and

9

pointed us toward the restrooms.

"I'll take him," Mitchell said.

"What a lovely beginning to our evening of romance," I replied.

"Why don't you comb your hair?" Mitchell pointed to the door of the ladies' room.

"Does it need it?" I felt around my head.

"No. But when you look in the mirror and see how pretty you look, it might make you feel better."

"Oh, Mitchell . . ." I felt better already.

We were shown to a table next to a window. A waiter in a frilly white shirt with black garters on his sleeves asked us if we wanted anything to drink.

"A martini," Zach piped up. "Very dry, shaken, not stirred."

The waiter grinned. "Cute kid."

"You won't think so in an hour," I said.

"We have some special *Queen of the Bay* soft drinks," he said. "I bet he'd like a Steamboat Willie."

"What's a Steamboat Willie?" Zach asked.

"It's named after Mickey Mouse's first cartoon," the waiter replied.

"I don't want to drink anything with a mouse in it!" Zach yelled.

I put my head in my hands.

When the rest of the passengers had boarded the boat, a voice on the loudspeaker introduced himself as the captain and welcomed us to the *Queen of the Bay*.

"State law requires that we follow certain regulations for the safety and comfort of our passengers."

"Just like an airplane," Zach said.

Life preservers were stowed beneath benches under the windows. I lifted up the lid of the bench next to us and saw a stack of orange life preservers.

"She always checks under her seat on planes, too," Zach said.

"No," I corrected him. "I check under *your* seat, hoping you won't have one."

"Let's go out on deck and watch them cast off," Mitchell suggested.

We went outside onto the lower deck. People lined the railings waiting for the boat to embark.

The sun was beginning to turn orange. The water took on a golden glow, and the air was soft and fresh. Mitchell put his arm around my shoulder. "Happy anniversary," he said softly.

"Happy anniversary," I said. I made a silent

vow that in spite of Zach, I was going to do everything I could to make this an evening we would always remember.

The crew unwound the ropes that held the boat to the pier, the Dixieland music piped out from the speakers again, and two sharp whistles announced our departure.

We watched the pier recede, then turned to admire the expanse of Long Island Sound that curved out ahead of us.

"I'd like to have a boat," Mitchell said. "Then we could do this all the time."

"Well, we've got one for tonight," I said.

He pulled me close to him. "But there are all these people around." He kissed my ear.

"You're not going to do that icky stuff here!" Zach shrieked.

I sighed. "But only one I'd like to drown."

We went back inside to our table to order dinner.

It took ten minutes for Zach to find something on the menu that didn't sound yucky. Our waiter didn't think Zach was cute anymore.

After we gave our orders, we climbed to the second deck. There was a small dance floor in the center and a disc jockey playing tapes. There were already plenty of couples on the floor.

Zach protested vigorously that he didn't want to sit around and watch us dance. I forgot my vow to enjoy the evening. I snapped.

"You brat! Why don't you just get lost? Why don't you do me a favor and drop off the edge of the earth!" I barely managed to keep from bursting into tears.

"Let me handle this," Mitchell said calmly. He took Zach aside.

I turned to watch the people on the dance floor slow dancing to a soft, lush number, unencumbered by seven-year-olds, involved only with each other. How I envied them.

There was a couple who had to be in their seventies, holding each other closely, swaying with the music, whispering to each other. They seemed as much in love as two people of any age could be.

I wished I were seventy. Childless. With no siblings.

Suddenly Mitchell's arms were around me and he was swirling me into the center of the floor. "A time for us . . ." he hummed along with the music.

I looked over his shoulder and saw Zach sitting against the wall, hands folded in his lap, absolutely still.

"We've got half an hour," Mitchell whispered into my ear. "Let's make the most of it."

"How did you do it?" I wrapped my arms around him.

"I know how to talk to kids." He stroked my hair. "And I paid him five bucks."

It was a wonderful half hour.

When the DJ put on some old sixties rock, we decided it was time for dinner. We looked over to where Zach had been sitting. Zach wasn't there.

I peered across the dance floor. I didn't see him anywhere.

"Oh, great," I said. "Where do you suppose he disappeared to?"

"I don't know," said Mitchell grimly, "but I want my five bucks back."

"Maybe he went downstairs to eat," I suggested. We circled the top deck to make sure he wasn't outside, then went down to the dining room.

Our food was there, but Zach wasn't.

"I'll check the bathroom," Mitchell said. "Why don't you look around the other tables and see if he found another kid to hang out with."

"Mitchell, couldn't we just sit down and have

our dinner in peace and be thankful that he's not hassling us?"

"No," he said, "we couldn't. We're responsible for him."

"You are so annoying," I grumbled. "Why did you have to choose tonight of all nights to act responsible?"

I crisscrossed the dining room trying to look as if I were on a casual stroll. But it was hard to look casual when I had to keep ducking my head under tables to see if Zach was hiding somewhere. There weren't many people seated yet, but those who were probably wondered about my peculiar interest in their feet.

"He's not in the bathroom," Mitchell said, catching up with me near the door to the outer deck. "And he's not at the bar trying to order a martini. They didn't see him."

"Well, he's got to be somewhere," I said impatiently. "This isn't a very large boat. He'll turn up."

"Dana, we're in the middle of Long Island Sound. We can't just wait for him to turn up. We have to know whether he's on the boat *now*."

My stomach lurched. "You don't think — he couldn't have — "

15

Mitchell put his arm around my shoulder and pulled me close. "No, no, of course not," he said quickly. "But that's why we're going to keep on looking. So we can enjoy the rest of the cruise without worrying."

"It's too late for that," I said miserably. "I'm really sorry about this, Mitchell."

"Hey, don't worry. Everything's going to be all right." He managed a weak smile. "One way or another, this is going to be a night to remember."

"That's what they called it when the *Titanic* sank."

We searched the lower deck separately, starting on opposite ends, so we couldn't miss Zach if he was moving around.

The sun had set, but Japanese lanterns strung overhead provided enough light to see everyone on deck. I looked out at the water, no longer glistening with gold tinges, but inky, cold, and forbidding.

I strained my eyes, terrified that I would spot a small, pale face bobbing in the Sound — and terrified that I wouldn't.

It had gotten much cooler, but I was shivering more from fear than from the temperature. Frantic, I started to run around the deck, yanking open doors marked DO NOT ENTER,

CREW ONLY, NO ADMITTANCE.

Zach wasn't behind any of them.

And no one behind them had seen a little boy come in.

I literally ran into Mitchell as I rounded the stern.

"Hey, hey." He caught me by the shoulders. "Take it easy. I talked to one of the crew and they're going to make an announcement over the PA system. The DJ will make one, too. Zach'll hear it, no matter where he is."

I looked out over the water. I didn't have to say what I was thinking.

"Dana, no." Mitchell pulled me toward the door to the dining room. "Someone would have seen him. There are people all over the place. He couldn't have fallen overboard."

Leaning against him, I went back inside. The dining room was a blur. I couldn't think, couldn't breathe, could barely hear the captain summoning Zach over the speaker system.

I sank into a chair at the edge of the dining area. A gray-haired man in a tuxedo came over and started talking to Mitchell. I didn't hear what he said, but I could tell from the expression of concern on his face that they hadn't found Zach.

I lowered my head and stared at my hands.

They looked so far away. And I couldn't feel my fingers, even though they were tightly clenched into fists. They didn't seem real. Nothing seemed real. Maybe because I didn't want it to be.

Suddenly I heard a shrill voice say something about hide-and-seek. I looked up. A little boy in a red jacket was talking to Mitchell. A woman in a blue dress stood next to them.

". . . and then my mother said it was time to eat, and I couldn't find him, so I went to eat."

Mitchell smiled radiantly. "Dana," he said, pulling me out of the chair, "they were just playing hide-and-seek. This boy and Zach — "

"But where is he?" I asked.

"I don't know." The boy in the red jacket shrugged. "I told you, I couldn't find him."

"I guess he's still hiding," Mitchell said.

"For an hour?" I said. "That's crazy. Zach could never be that patient. And he would have heard his name over the loudspeakers. He's not still hiding — he's still *lost*."

"Maybe if someone announced Ollie Ollie Oxen Freeo," Mitchell said. "He's a pretty stubborn kid."

"What are we going to *do*?" I cried.

The gray-haired man eyed me nervously.

"Please don't worry. I'm going to get all the available crew members and we'll search the boat completely. They're thoroughly familiar with every inch of — "

"We already searched the boat," I cut in. "He's not on the boat. What you should do is stop the boat and start dragging the Sound for his body!"

"Please," the man repeated, "he couldn't have gone overboard. We have crew at seven watch stations. There's no way anyone can have an accident on this boat without one of those people seeing it."

"There isn't?" I swallowed hard. "You mean, he really couldn't have fallen overboard?"

The man shook his head. "I assure you, it would be impossible. Now, why don't you just go back to your table and leave everything to us."

"Our table!" Mitchell smacked himself against the forehead. "Of course!"

"What are you? — "

But he was already sprinting toward our table. I hurried after him.

I reached him just as he grabbed the edge of the white cloth. "It's the one place we didn't look," he said. He lifted the tablecloth.

"See!" he said triumphantly.

But Zach wasn't there. Mitchell was pointing to a jumbled heap of life preservers that someone must have shoved under our table.

"What are they doing there?" I wondered. "They're supposed to be . . ."

"Exactly!" Mitchell dove for the bench where the life preservers were stowed. He lifted the lid. There, scrunched up in a heap, knees under his chin, rear end in the air, was Zach. Sound asleep.

"Zach!" I cried.

He opened his eyes slowly, lashes fluttering. For a moment he looked confused. Then he raised his head, put his finger to his lips, and whispered, "*Shh.* I'm hiding."

"The game's over." Mitchell reached for his arm. "The whole boat's been looking for you."

"They were?" Zach woke up all the way.

"They certainly were."

"Then I hid good, didn't I?" Zach said proudly.

Mitchell hauled him out of the cabinet, lowered the lid, and plopped him onto the bench. He squatted in front of him so they were at eye level.

"Your sister was very worried about you," he said sternly.

"She was?" Zach looked surprised. "Why?"

"You disappeared for an hour," Mitchell said.

"That long?" Zach's face lit up. "Then you owe me another five dollars!"

Mitchell still throws paper airplanes at me when I'm trying to study, and buys concert tickets for groups nobody's ever heard of.

But, as he pointed out, if he were not in touch with the childlike part of himself, he wouldn't have figured out where Zach was.

And he has changed. He doesn't come late anymore. He always meets me where he's supposed to and never keeps me wondering where he is, or when he'll show up.

"After what you went through because of Zach," he tells me, every time I marvel about his newfound punctuality, "I don't ever want you to feel uncertain about *me*."

"Love stuff again." Zach will make a disgusting face. *"Yucckk."*

"You little monster." I'll glower at him in my most menacing, big-sister fashion. "Get lost, will you?"

And Mitchell will clap his hands over Zach's ears and warn, "Don't listen to her, Zach! Whatever you do, don't get lost!"

And Zach will start to giggle, and Mitchell will start to giggle, and he'll eye me like a mischievous child trying to figure out how much he can get away with.

"You're as immature as Zach!" I'll scold him. "I can't stand either of you! I wish you'd both get lost!"

And they will. I'll stand there alone, seething, while they go off to play ball in the backyard, or bicker over their favorite Flintstone in the family room.

And maybe, about an hour later, Mitchell will emerge from the yard, or the family room, and spend some time with *me*.

So even though he's a little more considerate than he used to be, Mitchell Proctor is still the most annoying (full-grown) male in the world.

But I love him.

LIVERWURST AND ROSES

Howie Freel didn't know the exact moment that he'd fallen in love with Bonnie Fitzgerald, but the thing was, he had. He didn't know why like had turned to love, how friendship had blossomed into romance, or when the kid he'd known since they were first-grade babies had magically developed into a first-class babe.

And the other thing was, Bonnie didn't know it, either.

He was sure she had no idea that when she said, "Hi, Freel," as she always did, his knees turned to Jell-O. She didn't know what a struggle it was to keep his voice normal when he answered, "Hi, Fitz."

She didn't know the iron self-control it took

to walk her home after school without throwing his arms around her and plastering her gorgeous face with kisses.

And she certainly showed no desire to plaster his face with kisses. She showed no desire for him whatsoever. He was just good old Howie, best buddy, great sense of humor, zero hunk quotient.

Not knowing what to do with his turbulent feelings, Howie kept them to himself. He suffered in silence, maintaining the relationship the way it had always been, afraid if he pushed for something closer, he might lose her entirely.

But the situation reached an intolerable level when Bonnie started to date. Other guys. Guys with considerable hunk quotient. Guys who probably weren't afraid to snuggle up to her in the movies, or plaster her face with kisses when they took her home.

Bonnie didn't tell him the gory details, but his imagination ran wild every time she went out with one of them.

At this point Howie could suffer in silence no longer.

"I can't stand it," he told Jon Kramer. They were shooting hoops in Jon's driveway. Howie blew six foul shots in a row. When Jon asked him what was wrong, he blurted out everything. "Every time I see her with another guy, I want to open a vein," he said.

"Does she know you like her?" asked Jon.

"Like her?" Howie repeated. "*Like* her? I don't just 'like' her, Kramer. I *love* her. With a deep, burning, eternal flame of passion."

"That's pretty poetic," said John, impressed. "Why don't you tell her that?"

"I can't tell her that! I can hardly say hello to her without keeling over."

"Then write it," Jon said. "Girls really go for those flowery love letters."

"Write her a love letter?" Even thinking about it made Howie panicky. "That seems pretty drastic."

"Who's she going out with tonight?" asked Jon.

"Dexter Brevitch," Howie answered glumly.

"The wrestler?" Jon tossed the basketball at Howie's head. "Don't you think drastic steps are called for?"

The ball grazed Howie's ear. He hardly felt it. He thought of Dexter's meaty arm around Bonnie's slim waist, his broken nose nuzzling her delicate ear. He closed his eyes as if he could shut out the hideous image. But he couldn't switch off his imagination. His stomach churned, and prickles of sweat broke out on his upper lip.

"But what if she laughs in my face?" he asked.

"How can she laugh in your face?" Jon said. "You'll mail her the letter, she'll read it in private, and if she does laugh, you'll never know it."

"But what's the point?" Howie asked. "To her we're just friends. One mushy letter isn't going to change her mind."

"How do you know?" Jon demanded. "Maybe she feels the same way you do. Maybe she's just waiting for you to make the first move."

"Why would she wait?" said Howie. "Bonnie was never shy."

"Neither were you until you fell in love with her."

Howie sighed. "Well, I'll think about it." He headed down the driveway, shoulders slumping.

"Don't think about it too long," Jon called after him. "Those wrestlers know some pretty fancy holds."

Howie's stomach turned over again.

Dear Bonnie,
This is a hard letter to write . . .
(This is an impossible letter to write.)
For a long time, unbeknownst to you . . .
(Unbeknownst? *Unbeknownst?* Freel, are
    you nuts?)
You light up my life . . .
(Oh, puh-leeze!)

Howie ripped up the three sheets of paper
and tossed the pieces into the air. They rained
down on him like a shower of shattered hopes.

What made him think he could write a love
letter? He'd never gotten higher than a C+ in
English.

He picked up his guitar and began to strum
a mournful series of chords. He wasn't a great
musician, but he felt that he compensated for
his lack of skill with an abundance of soul.

A song! Of course!

You could say anything you wanted in a
song. As long as you made it rhyme and set it
to music, you could talk about love and passion
without making a fool of yourself.

He got his tape recorder and sat down cross-
legged on the floor. He tuned his guitar and
waited for the creative juices to flow.

* * *

27

It took him one afternoon to write the song and record it. But it took him three days to work up the courage to give the tape to Bonnie.

"What is it?" she asked as he thrust the tape at her abruptly Friday afternoon.

"It's a song I wrote." He wanted to add, "for you," but he couldn't bring himself to say it.

But she'd know, as soon as she heard it. He wouldn't have to spell out his feelings for her. They were all there, in melody, in lyrics, in the key of G.

"I think of you in the morning when the sun begins to shine,
"I think of you in the evening when the stars come out at nine,
"I think of you the whole day through, how can I make you mine?
"Ooh ooh. Ooh ooh. Ooh ooh."

"Hey, Freel!" Dexter Brevitch approached him in the locker room before gym class. He was wearing only his jockey shorts. Every muscle in his body rippled as he confronted Howie. And that was a lot of muscle.

Uh-oh. Howie was glad that he was still dressed. If Dexter wanted to kill him for putting a move on Bonnie, at least he wouldn't have to flee the locker room naked.

He cringed against his locker, trying to look as if he wasn't cringing.

"That was a nice song you wrote," Dexter said unexpectedly. "I liked it."

"Uh, thanks." Howie relaxed a little. Dexter didn't sound as if he were about to kill him. But then he realized something.

"You heard it?" he asked.

"Oh, yeah. Bonnie and me listened to it Friday night. It's real — you know — romantic." Dexter gave him a playful punch on the shoulder. Howie bounced off the locker and staggered sideways. "I think you got talent."

Howie was so outraged, he ignored the pain in his shoulder. Bonnie had taken his song and played it for Dexter. She'd used his soulful declaration of love to set the mood for a sordid smooching session with this overdeveloped, steroid-swilling troglodyte.

"So, you gonna be a songwriter, or what?" Dexter asked.

I'll never write another song as long as I live, Howie vowed to himself.

But to Dexter he said, "I don't think so. I think I'll probably be a taxidermist."

* * *

"What a nightmare," he told Jon. "I pour out my heart in song and she uses it for make-out music with Dexter."

"I guess you have to be more direct," Jon said. "Apparently she didn't realize you were pouring out your heart."

"Oh, right," Howie retorted. " 'I think of you the whole day through, how can I make you mine?' is too subtle."

"Well, you didn't say, 'I think of you the whole day through, how can I make you mine, *Bonnie*,' " Jon said.

"Nothing rhymes with Bonnie." Howie put his head in his hands.

"Look," said Jon, "this is ridiculous. How does any guy approach a girl? Take her to a romantic restaurant, send her flowers, buy her a bracelet."

"I have twenty-seven dollars in the bank," Howie said.

"Take her to McDonald's," Jon snapped. "Buy her a *small* bracelet. You don't need money to let a girl know you like her. Just do something to show her how much."

"That was a cute song you wrote," said Bonnie. "Dexter really liked it."

They were sitting at their usual table in the

school cafeteria. Howie watched her poke at her chicken chow mein. It was, he realized, the perfect moment to reveal his feelings. She'd mentioned the song, so she must be curious about why he'd given it to her. And when he told her, she wouldn't laugh so hysterically that she'd choke on her food, because she wasn't eating any of it.

He took a deep breath. He cleared his throat. "I was — "

"This stuff is awful!" She shoved her plate away. "A liverwurst sandwich would taste like caviar compared to this."

"About my s — " he began again.

"I keep meaning to bring my own lunch," she grumbled. "But I never seem to have time in the morning."

Howie pushed half his sandwich toward her. He reached into his brown bag and took out an apple and two oatmeal cookies.

"Here. Listen, I wanted to tell — "

"Howie, I can't," she protested. "You'll be starving all day."

"I don't mind." He swallowed hard. "See, I — "

"Well, maybe just one cookie." She bit into the oatmeal cookie and delicately licked the crumbs from her lips.

Such courage as Howie had mustered dissolved faster than a spoonful of sugar in a cup of scalding tea.

"Mmm, heavenly," said Bonnie. Her voice was deep and velvety.

Howie nearly passed out.

The idea hit him on the way home, as he was listening to his stomach rumble. Bonnie had eaten the cookie, the apple, and finally accepted part of his sandwich.

He could make her a special lunch, and surprise her with it the next day. He might even gift-wrap the sandwich, put everything in a bag, and tie a fancy bow to it, like a present.

Well, maybe the bow was too much.

A rose! he thought. One perfect rose. A liverwurst sandwich, a pickle, some cookies, and a rose. She would marvel at how thoughtful he was, how much he cared about her. She'd eat the lunch, smell the rose, and know that only someone who loved her very deeply would go to so much trouble.

He headed downtown. "Buds Я Us" wouldn't be open in time for him to buy the rose tomorrow morning. It would keep in the refrigerator overnight.

When he got to the flower shop, he was the

only customer. A blonde girl behind the counter looked up from her paperback. She was tall and thin and wore earrings that looked like turkey bones, which hung down nearly to her shoulders.

"I want one perfect rose," he said.

"What color?" the girl asked.

"Red."

"Okey doke." She went to a glass refrigerated case and picked out a red rose. She held it out to him. It *was* a perfect rose. It was a magnificent rose.

"That'll be four dollars."

"Four dollars!" For the second time that day Howie nearly passed out.

"They're cheaper if you buy them by the dozen," she said. "But for one perfect rose it's four bucks."

"What about one imperfect rose?" Howie asked desperately.

"They're all the same price," she said. "A rose is a rose is a rose." She grinned at him. "That's a florist joke."

"Ha ha." Howie walked dejectedly out of "Buds Я Us." He couldn't spend four dollars on a rose.

Across the street, in Woolworth's window, he spotted a display of artificial flowers. Maybe a plastic rose would be okay. It was still a romantic gesture, even if it wasn't a real rose. It was the thought that counted.

Besides, he tried to convince himself, a real rose would be dead in a couple of days. This rose would live forever. Every time Bonnie looked at it, she would think of him.

After all, a rose is a rose is a rose, he told himself.

He crossed the street and went into Woolworth's.

He didn't get to walk to school much with Bonnie anymore. Dexter drove her, and when he didn't have afternoon matches, he drove her home, too.

Things were reaching a crisis point. If this romantic lunch didn't work, he didn't know what he'd do. Maybe drop out of school and become a monk.

He got up half an hour early to prepare Bonnie's lunch. The plastic rose had cost eighty-nine cents. At the supermarket he'd bought liverwurst, a sourdough French baguette, and a huge Comice pear. He'd never heard of Comice pears, but they were $2.19 a pound, so he figured they must be pretty special.

Fortunately there was a Pepperidge Farm

carrot cake in his freezer. He hacked two slices from the cake, using a bread knife driven by a meat-tenderizing mallet. The slices were pretty ragged-looking, but they would still taste good when they thawed out.

The rose was too long to fit in the bag. He could Scotch tape it to the outside, but he'd feel a little self-conscious carrying a lunch bag with a flower on it.

He hated to cut it — but he would have hated it more if he were cutting the four-dollar rose. So he lopped three inches off it and put it in the bag. It didn't look very elegant with its stem shortened, but then, it hadn't looked all that elegant to begin with.

At lunchtime Bonnie was already sitting at their table. He was sure that the only reason she still ate lunch with him was because Dexter had a different lunch period.

"Ms. Fitzgerald," he said, bowing low. Keep it light, Freel, he warned himself. "Your tragic plight moved me."

Bonnie looked at him curiously. "What tragic plight?"

"Your lunch plight. Therefore I have — "

"Oh." She grinned. "It moved me, too." She reached into her backpack and pulled out a brown paper bag. "It moved me to take your advice. I got up early and made my own lunch."

"You what?" Howie stood there stupidly, holding two lunch bags, unable to make his mouth form any more words. Hastily he tried to stick one of the bags behind his back. But he wasn't fast enough.

"Oh, Howie, did you make me lunch?"

He nodded.

"What a sweet thing to do."

"But obviously," he said, "pointless."

"Not at all," she protested. "I'll bet you made me a much nicer lunch than I brought. I just have a liverwurst sandwich. Howie, what's the matter?"

How could he have been so dumb? If he were going to make a gallant gesture, like preparing her lunch, why hadn't he made it something wonderful? Like smoked turkey with honey mustard? Or roast beef and Muenster cheese with horseradish dressing? Or —

Because liverwurst or bologna was all he could afford, and because she had told him that she'd rather have liverwurst than caviar. Well, she'd said something like that.

She reached for one of the bags.

"You've already got lunch," he said. "You don't want this."

"Yes I do," she insisted. "Come on, Howie,

36

it was a lovely gesture. And I'm really hungry today."

He shoved the bag at her. "Fine. Now you have two liverwurst sandwiches."

"You made liverwurst, too?" She laughed delightedly. "What a funny coincidence."

"Hilarious," he said.

She opened the bag. "A rose! Howie, you put a rose in my lunch!" She pulled out the plastic flower and admired it. "What a sweet thing to do."

"Yeah. Sweet."

"Well, it is," she said. "And I certainly didn't bring myself a flower." She bent the rose and stuck it into her hair behind her ear. "I feel quite glamorous," she said.

I feel like a jerk, Howie thought.

"Hey, Howie, want to shoot some hoops?" Jon was on the phone.

"I want to shoot myself," Howie replied.

"Aww, you're not going to start this again, are you?"

"Listen carefully, Jon. I made a complete fool of myself. I don't ever want to eat lunch again."

"In our cafeteria that's the first rule of survival," Jon said.

"She was laughing at me."

"No she wasn't," Jon argued. "She wore that rose in her hair all day. She told everyone that you gave it to her."

"So everyone could laugh at me."

"Wrong, wrong, wrong," Jon said. "She wore it because it made her feel happy. Now if you would just tell her — "

"I have to hang up," Howie cut in. "I'm going to jump out a second-story window and kill myself."

"Freel, you live in a ranch house."

"So I'll go next door."

The following day Howie ate lunch in the locker room. On Thursday he took his lunch to the football field and ate in the bleachers.

Friday morning he opened his front door to find Bonnie standing on the steps. Her arms were folded across her chest, and the expression on her face was grim.

"Freel, why are you avoiding me?"

"I'm not avoiding you," he lied.

"Then why don't you eat lunch with me anymore? Why don't you talk to me anymore? Why don't I see you anymore?"

"Because you're always with Dexter," he said.

"Not at lunchtime. What's with you? You give a girl a sandwich and a rose and you never talk to her again? Do you always give girls flowers before you dump them?"

"Dump you?" he said. "*I* dumped *you*?"

"Well, what do you call it when you stop speaking to someone? When you look the other way when you see them coming?"

"Self-defense," Howie said miserably.

"What?" She searched his face. Her eyes were wide and her lips trembled. She looked very vulnerable. "Don't you want to be friends anymore?" she whispered.

He finally lost it. "No!" he shouted. "No, I don't!"

Her eyes filled with tears. "But why? What did I do?"

He'd never seen her so hurt. He hated himself.

"Nothing!" he snapped. "Don't you understand? I *like* you."

She wiped her eyes with her fingers. "You like me? You sure have a funny way of showing it."

He dropped his books to the lawn. He put his hands on her shoulders. He took a deep breath. "I mean, I *like* you. Really like you. More than a friend."

"Oh." Her eyes widened in comprehension. *"Ohh."*

"But I know you don't feel the same way. And I made a fool of myself trying to show you. So for the sake of my mental health and emotional well-being — "

"Why didn't you tell me?" she demanded.

"I tried," he said. "I brought you lunch, I gave you a rose, I wrote you a song . . ."

"I didn't know you wrote that song for me," she said. "I just thought — well, I thought it was a joke."

"A *joke*?" Angrily he snatched his books from the lawn and stalked toward the street.

She hurried after him. "Howie, wait. I mean, I thought it was a sort of a parody. You know, that ooh ooh part. I didn't realize — "

His face was hot with humiliation. There had been other moments in his life when he'd thought, This is the worst thing that ever happened to me. But every one of them paled in comparison to this.

"Howie, please." She caught up to him and grabbed his arm. "If I knew you meant it for me, do you think I would have played it in front of Dexter?"

"Dexter loved it," Howie said bitterly. "He thought it was real romantic."

"Oh, Howie. Why didn't you just tell me?"

"How could I?" He stopped in the middle of the sidewalk. "What if you laughed at me? What if we had to stop being friends after I told you? Then I'd never get to see you. And I knew you didn't like me *that* way."

"How did you know I didn't?" Bonnie asked softly.

"Because you never told me you did."

"And you never told me," she replied.

Howie's heart lurched. He felt the blood rushing to his head so fast that he thought his corpuscles might explode in his veins.

"You mean — are you saying — "

"I'm saying it's hard to change a relationship," Bonnie answered. "I'm saying that you've always been fun and I love your sense of humor."

"I'm a million laughs," Howie said.

"So how was I supposed to know you weren't just joking around?" she asked. "Like you always do? Like we always did?"

"Bonnie . . ." He wished she'd come right out and say whatever it was she was getting at. He didn't want to hope, and he couldn't bear not to.

"Why did you go out with Dexter?" he asked. It was the only thing he could think of to say. "And all those other guys?"

"They asked me," she said simply. "And I thought maybe if I started going out, you'd look at me differently."

He could hardly see straight. The street disappeared, the houses disappeared, everything around him misted over like morning fog. Only Bonnie's face was clear. Bonnie's beautiful face.

"You should have told me," he said.

"Freel, you're the last person to criticize me for not telling you."

"You really like me?" he asked incredulously. "Really, really like me?"

"I really like you," she said.

Stunned, Howie gazed down at her. Should he kiss her? Should he hug her? Should he throw his books in the air and shout, "YES!"?

Bonnie was his, at last, and he had no idea what his next move was supposed to be.

"What do we do now?" he asked finally.

"We walk to school," she said. She pressed her fingers against his palm. "Holding hands."

ARNOLD BING,
THE CARPET KING

Anyone who's ever driven on Route 44 from Walpurgis to the state capital knows who my father is. His signs line the highway for miles north and south of town. There's a big picture of him wearing a smile and a crown. ARNOLD BING, THE CARPET KING! the letters scream out at passing motorists. RUGS FIT FOR A RAJAH AT PRICES THAT WON'T MAKE YOU A PAUPER!

Until I was seven years old I thought my father really was a king. I mean, how else could you explain the crown? But by the time I hit puberty, his sales pitches had begun to embarrass me.

I still cringe when I see him on our local cable

station, wearing that stupid crown and showing the viewers around his Castle of Carpets.

But something happened to make me take an interest in my father's business. That something was named Garrett Cullum.

Garrett Cullum was tall, dark, with intense brown eyes that grew even more intense when he discussed . . . carpets. He was a freshman marketing major at Walpurgis Community College, and he thought my father was a genius.

He went to work for him not for the puny salary, but because he said he wanted to learn P.R. (Public Relations) and M.&M. (Merchandising and Marketing) from a master.

Garrett tends to talk in initials a lot. "Even if I end up in A.&R. (Artists and Repertoire) or R.&D. (Research and Development)," he told my mother at dinner one night, "this kind of hands-on experience will be invaluable."

I don't know what it was that plunged me so deeply in love with Garrett — except for his incredible good looks — but from the moment my father introduced us that night, I couldn't take my eyes off him.

I assumed it was pure physical attraction. Why else would I spend the entire dinner hanging on Garrett's every word? Every word he uttered had to do with . . . carpets.

Buying them, selling them, advertising them, installing them in odd-shaped rooms, cutting them into irregular sizes, using outdoor carpets indoors, industrial-quality floor coverings on residential floors.

"Why didn't you tell me about him?" I asked my father after Garrett left that night.

"You were never that interested in the business," he replied.

"I'm still not that interested . . ." I muttered, ". . . in the business."

But I took to hanging around the store a lot, dropping in on various lame pretenses, dragging in my friend Erica to check him out, helping to write up orders during Broadloom Bonanza week.

"I don't know what you see in him, Laurel," Erica remarked, after meeting Garrett. "I mean, okay, he's incredibly handsome, but all he can think about is . . . carpets."

"Conversation is overrated," I said. "There are better ways to communicate."

You'd think that Garrett would have jumped at the chance to cement his relationship with my father by showing a little interest in the boss's daughter.

You would be wrong.

Garrett showed no interest in anything except M.&M., P.R., and S.Y. (square yards). D.D.'s (delivery dates) were the only kind of dates he arranged.

L.B. (Laurel Bing) was getting nowhere, P.D.Q.

Until my father announced that he was going to sponsor a beauty contest to pick Miss Floor Covering.

"That is the dumbest thing I ever heard," I said. "Beauty pageants are sexist exploitations of young, innocent women that give lecherous old men an excuse to ogle female flesh."

"It was Garrett's idea," my father said.

"Although if handled in good taste," I added hastily, "they can be wholesome opportunities for deserving girls to win scholarships."

"Right." My father nodded. "That's the way I see it. Of course, I can't give anybody a scholarship. But I figure the honor of being Miss Floor Covering, and riding in the Walpurgis Day parade, will be reward enough."

I had my doubts about that, but I didn't want to say anything that might undermine Garrett's relationship with my father. At least, not until he established a relationship with me.

"You might be right," I said. "Walpurgis Day is a big deal. I suppose a lot of girls would be excited about being in the parade."

"I'm glad you feel that way." He looked relieved. "Because I entered you in the contest."

"You *what*?"

"Why are you screaming like that? You just said lots of girls would be excited — "

"But I'm not one of them!" I screamed. "I don't want to be in a stupid beauty contest with a stupid name like Miss Floor Covering."

"But, Laurel — "

"Geez, it's a good thing you don't sell fertilizer," I said. "Imagine what you'd call — "

"Laurel, stop shouting at your father," my mother cut in.

"I'll stop as soon as he tells me I don't have to be in the contest!" I shouted.

"But I already nominated you," he insisted.

"Un-nominate me!"

"All right, all right." He sighed. "But this is a big disappointment to me, Laurel. Just when I thought you were taking an interest in the business. I'd hoped it would be a real family affair. Me, the Carpet King, you, a contestant, Garrett, one of the judges, Mom, decorating the car — "

"Whoa! Back up," I said. "Garrett's going to be one of the judges?"

"That's right. Since it was his idea, I thought it only fair — "

"Will the contestants have to — um — spend a lot of time with the judges?" I tried to sound casual. My mother's lips twitched. I guess I didn't sound casual enough.

"The way Garrett planned it, there'll be informal personal interviews and a luncheon for all the contestants and judges."

How many personal interviews? I wondered. And just how personal could we get?

"What about bathing suits?" I asked. I don't like bathing suits. I have too much on the bottom and not enough on the top.

"No bathing suits," he said.

"Talent competition?" I can't sing, dance, act, or twirl a baton. I'm good in chemistry, but how far would that get me in a talent contest? What could I do, recite the periodic table of the elements?

"No talent competition," he said. "Just poise and personality. We want a regular, All-American girl."

Well, I have a personality. And I'm American.

"But what about favoritism?" I asked. "I mean, how would it look for your daughter to — "

"You mean, you *will* do it?" His eyes lit up. "You won't make me un-nominate you?"

"I didn't say that. I'm just asking a few exploratory questions. Wouldn't people think the contest was fixed if I won?"

Not that I wanted to win. In fact, I could think of nothing I would hate more than riding in a parade with a cardboard crown on my head and a train made out of a stair runner and a "Miss Floor Covering" sash across my chest.

But if I was in the contest, Garrett would have to notice me. And pay attention to me.

"No one will think the contest is fixed," my father said. "For one thing, school averages are going to count for one third of the scoring. For another, we've chosen judges whose integrity is above reproach."

He told me who the judges were. Stalton Snow, the mayor of Walpurgis. Lydia Walpurgis, great-great-grandniece of the founder of the town. Garrett, of course, and Athena Untermeyer.

Ms. Untermeyer. My phys. ed. teacher. Who gave me D's four marking periods in a row. Who said she'd never had a student with a worse attitude in thirty years of teaching. With her as one of the judges, and with my PE grades dragging my average down, there was no chance I'd end up in the Walpurgis Day parade with a cardboard crown, stair-runner train, and a "Miss Floor Covering" sash across my chest.

But there was a good chance I'd see a lot of Garrett.

"I'll do it," I said. "When do we get up close and personal with the judges?"

To nominate someone for Miss Floor Covering, you had to go to the Castle of Carpets and fill out an official ballot. With his usual wild enthusiasm, my father had six hundred ballots printed up. When the deadline for entries passed, he had five hundred and eighty-one ballots left over.

The nineteen contestants and the judges met for the first time two weeks before the parade. The contestants, all from Walpurgis High, sat on rug remnants on the Castle floor. The judges sat on folding chairs in front of the vinyl tile display.

I looked around at my competitors as we waited for my father to begin his introductory remarks. And I realized I had made a hideous mistake.

Why hadn't it occurred to me that the girls most likely to enter a beauty contest were girls who belonged in a beauty contest? They weren't all drop-dead gorgeous, but the harsh truth was that most of them were far better-looking than me.

Even as my father explained that poise and personality, along with school grades, counted for seventy-five percent of the judging, depression smothered me like a mildewed blanket.

Garrett had already been exposed to my personality. As for poise — well, he'd seen me juggle customers during Broadloom Bonanza week. My P.&P. hadn't made the slightest impression on him. Was he likely to care much about my G.P.A. (grade point average)?

So here I was, the least glamorous of all the girls he'd be spending the next fourteen days with, and I expected him to notice me *now*?

I tuned out the rest of the meeting. I haven't the slightest idea what my father said, or what Garrett said, or what any of the other contestants said.

All I remember is what I said when I got home.

"I changed my mind about the contest. Un-nominate me."

My father looked stunned. "Why?"

"Did you see all those other girls?" I demanded. "I can't possibly win."

"I got the impression you didn't want to win," my mother said.

"That's not the point," I said. "It was stupid of me to agree to do it. I don't belong in a beauty contest, and I want out."

"It's too late to get out," my father objected. "I've already given the names of the contestants to *W.W.*"

W.W. is *Walpurgis Week*, our local newspaper. My father was beginning to talk like Garrett.

"I don't care," I said stubbornly. "I'm not going to do it."

"Laurel, you can't do this to me!" he shouted. "How would it look if the King's own daughter refused to — "

"You're not a king!" I retorted. "You can't order people around."

"I'm your father!" he snapped. "I can order *you* around."

"Arnold," my mother coaxed. "Laurel, please."

"Behead me!" I shot back. "I'm not following this order."

I stormed off to my room. I climbed into bed fully dressed and cried for fifteen minutes. Five minutes because of the fight with my father, five minutes because I didn't look like

Miss America, and five minutes because Garrett would never love me.

Things were tense at breakfast the next morning. My father read the *W.W.* article about the contest out loud, including the list of all the contestants. He read my name last, shook his head, and slapped the paper down on the table. He glared at me as if I were some sort of carpet spy, divulging vital broadloom specifications to enemy rug dealers.

He didn't actually call me a traitor to the Castle, but he did sigh deeply, stare down at his bowl of raisin bran, and murmur, " 'How sharper than a serpent's tooth it is to have a thankless child.' "

When I didn't respond, he added, "Shakespeare. Spoken by another king whose daughter disappointed him."

For the next two weeks I kept myself busy trying to forget Garrett, who would never love me, and ignoring the contest, which I was no longer in. I didn't go anywhere near the Castle of Carpets.

I resolved to learn five new words a day. I rented eleven tapes from the video store. I read through a stack of back issues of *Scientific*

American that I found in the garage. I made chicken soup for my father, who stayed home for four days with the flu.

We didn't speak much, but preparing soup from scratch gave me something to do.

I changed channels every time a commercial for the Castle appeared on TV.

The night before the parade, my father turned on the local news while we ate dinner. "I'm announcing the name of Miss Floor Covering tonight," he said. "We finished the judging yesterday."

"How can you do that?" I asked. "You're here."

"I taped it this afternoon." For some reason, he looked a bit uncomfortable.

"Well, who won?" my mother asked.

"Just watch," he said. "You'll find out in a moment."

And sure enough, my father's face appeared on the screen. The camera pulled back to show all four judges gathered behind him.

"I've just been handed this sealed envelope," my father on TV said. He held it up to the camera. "The envelope that contains the name of Walpurgis Day's first Miss Floor Covering."

He ripped open the envelope and pulled out

a sheet of paper. "And the winner is — " his whole face lit up, glowing with pride and delight — "Laurel Bing!"

"WHAT?" I leaped up from my chair, knocking over a water glass and sending my plate and silverware crashing to the floor.

"How could I have won?" I shrieked. "I wasn't in it! I didn't go to the luncheon! I didn't meet the judges!"

"Laurel, stop screaming at your father." But my mother didn't say it very forcefully. She seemed as shocked as I was.

"You got the majority of the popular vote," my father said.

"What popular vote?" I demanded. "I thought the judging was on poise, personality, and grades. Who got to vote?"

"Didn't you see the new commercials?" he asked. "Anyone who came to the Castle could cast a ballot. Garrett thought it would bring in a lot of customers. So we decided to have the popular vote count for one third."

"But how could people have voted for me if I wasn't in the contest?" I persisted.

"And your school average helped."

"My average is average!" I shot back. "You're avoiding my question."

He looked down at his hands. "Garrett re-entered you when I was home sick. I didn't find out till I went back to the Castle on Wednesday."

"I won't do it! It's fixed, and everyone will know it. Garrett must have stuffed the ballot box, or bribed the judges — or *something*."

"What would he bribe them with?" my mother asked. "And why?"

"To please the King," I said bitterly. "That's all he ever wanted to do. He probably planned this right from the beginning, to get in good with Dad. There's no way I could have won this contest honestly."

"That's ridiculous, Laurel," my father said. "You won fair and square, and you're going to be Miss Floor Covering."

"I did not choose to run! I can't fulfill the obligations of Miss Floor Covering. The first runner-up will have to take over."

"There is no first runner-up," he said. "You are Miss Floor Covering, and you *will* ride in the parade, if I have to drag you there kicking and screaming."

I faced him, my eyes cold with rage, my heart hot with rebellion. "I will never, *ever* make you chicken soup again."

*   *   *

The parade assembled at the American Legion Hall on the outskirts of town. My father dragged me there, kicking and screaming.

Girl Scouts, marching bands, baton twirlers, clowns, and fire engines clamored around us as the line of march organized.

I was extremely ungracious and totally unregal as my father perched me on top of the backseat of a 1957 Cadillac convertible. Banners reading MISS FLOOR COVERING were draped across both sides of the car.

He stuck a stupid plastic crown on my head and adjusted a fake red velvet and ermine cape around my shoulders. We were positioned about midway in the line of march, between the Police Department bagpipe band, and Troop 129 of the Boy Scouts.

My father wore his crown, too, as he settled on the top of the seat next to me. Garrett sat behind the wheel.

"Just smile and wave," my father instructed me. He pointed to a large plastic trash bag on the seat. "And toss out carpet samples to the crowd."

"Carpet samples? You want me to throw carpet samples?"

"Our new fall colors," he said. "And Tootsie

Rolls for the kids. They're in the smaller bag."

"This is a nightmare," I said.

"This is an *honor*," he argued. "Your attitude is a nightmare. Can't you just relax and try to have fun with the whole thing?"

I looked down at the fake fur trim of my cape. I felt the crown tilting awkwardly on my head. This was as close to being a beauty queen as I would ever come. No matter how I had won, I *had* won. I supposed there was a miniscule possibility that the competition had been legitimate.

And my father hadn't kept me in the contest. That was Garrett's doing.

I took a deep breath. I smiled at him for the first time in two weeks. "All right, your majesty. I'll try to be a worthy Miss Floor Covering."

He hugged me. "Oh, honey, I'm so proud of you."

"Watch out for my crown."

Finally our car began to move. The bagpipers marching in front of us made any further conversation impossible. We could see people lining both sides of Main Street as we crawled toward it.

My father pulled out a handful of two-inch-square carpet samples and dropped them into my lap. As we reached the first few spectators, I waved and tossed the bits of carpet to the cluster of people on the sidewalk.

My father threw out some Tootsie Rolls.

Three adults and two kids grabbed the samples as they hit the sidewalk. Yelling something we couldn't hear because of the bagpipers, they threw the carpet samples back at us.

One of the kids even threw back a Tootsie Roll.

The missiles landed harmlessly on the trunk lid, but my father's face turned white.

"What did they do that for?" he yelled in my ear.

"Maybe they don't like the new fall colors."

Garrett turned around and mouthed something at us. We couldn't hear what he said, but I think it was meant to be reassuring.

The crowds grew thicker as we reached the center of town. Thicker, louder, and uglier. I could hear them now, even over the unholy screeching of the bagpipers.

"FIX! FAKE! BOOOO!"

Half the samples I threw out came flying back at us. My father stopped tossing Tootsie Rolls. He was speechless, motionless. He sat next to me, stiff as a cardboard figure, his face frozen in shock.

Not everyone booed us. Some people even cheered and waved. I think they were mostly parents of the Boy Scouts marching behind us. I pretended they were cheering for me. I tried to smile graciously back.

But my heart felt like granite in my chest, and my cape couldn't hide my humiliation. I began tossing carpet samples and Tootsie Rolls wildly into the crowd, as if I could ward off their scorn with broadloom and chocolate.

Things reached a hideous crescendo as we drove past the Castle of Carpets. Through my tears I could see a group of the other contestants for Miss Floor Covering clustered on the sidewalk, surrounded by a jeering mob of their supporters.

Finally, my father came out of his stupor. He began to fling carpet samples and candy like a man possessed. "Fair and square!" he shouted back at the crowd. "Fair and square! Miss Floor Covering! The Princess of Carpets!"

I thought he'd lost his mind.

He was just making them angrier. Now everyone was pelting us with pieces of carpet. As fast as the King flung them out, they came flying back at the Cadillac, along with a torrent of Tootsie Rolls, a tomato that knocked my crown off, and a whole lot of eggs.

"Get down, Laurel!" he screamed. He pulled me to the floor of the car. He bundled my cape over me and shielded my body with his.

We huddled there together, hands covering our heads. I felt like a despised dictator on the eve of a revolution.

"How could I do this to you?" he groaned. "Laurel, I'm so sorry. This is the worst day of my whole life."

"I'm not having much fun, either," I agreed.

We lived through it. Even though Garrett had to drive the rest of the parade route with one hand on the steering wheel and his head ducked under it.

By the time we got back to the American Legion Hall, the Police Department bagpipers and the Boy Scouts hated us as much as everyone else. A lot of people with very bad aim had missed our car and hit the groups marching in front and behind us.

Fortunately, no one was hurt.

My father and I climbed out of the car, stiff from scrunching on the floor, bruised in spirit as well as body.

"Garrett," my father said, yanking open the driver-side door, "you're fired."

"But, A.B.!" he cried.

"Don't call me A.B. Don't call me King. Don't call me, *ever*. Get out of my sight. I'll mail you your final check."

"But she *won*," Garrett said. "Isn't that what you wanted?"

My father's eyes grew so fierce, I thought they would burn a hole through Garrett's heart. "I want only one thing," he said, his voice dangerously soft. "I want you to disappear."

He did.

It took us four days to get over the worst of the trauma. My mother had been inside the Castle, watching from the window, repeatedly dialing 911, and being told that most of the police were already at the parade, so there was nothing to worry about.

My friend Erica took it on herself to try and convince the other contestants that if the contest had been fixed, it wasn't me or my father who'd fixed it. At least one person in Walpurgis was still speaking to me.

As the shock wore off, my father began to realize what a blow his business had suffered. "A P.R. disaster," he moaned. "Ten years of goodwill, gone, all gone. How could I have *made* such a blunder?"

"This will die down," my mother tried to tell

him, when her headaches subsided. "You're still the King of Carpets."

"I lost my crown in the parade," he said sadly.

"I'll make you a new one," my mother promised.

"Thanks, hon." He put his arm around her and hugged her. "You're still my queen."

He pulled me into his other arm. "And you're still my princess," he said, his voice all mushy and sentimental. "And I promise, I'll never again force you to do anything you don't want to do."

I hugged him back. "I didn't mean what I said about the chicken soup," I told him.

Suddenly he let go of us. His eyes lit up — a dangerous sign that my mother and I both recognized.

"That's it! A whole new campaign! Family centered. We'll do the commercials together. The Royal Family of Carpets!"

"No!" I said. *"No!"*

"You'll be the Carpet Princess," he told me excitedly. "People will see how nice you really are — "

"No!" I backed away. "People hate me. You'll just make it worse."

"And you — " He turned to my mother.

"You'll be the Carpet Queen, with your crown, and — "

"No!" cried my mother, horrified.

"But we'll emphasize that beneath our royal robes and crowns, we're just a warm, close-knit American family." He burned with enthusiasm. "A chicken-soup kind of family. And our whole lives are dedicated to providing quality floor coverings for our loyal subjects."

"No, no, *no*!"

"Of course," he went on happily, "my crown will be the biggest. . . ."

BODY WAVE

Oh, good, Cheryl, you're ready for me.

Yes, I know how busy you've been. This is, like, a really, really major dance. I mean, next to the prom —

Oh, no, not with him. With Doug Malloy. It's a really weird story. I mean, I wanted Brent to ask me, and I was sure he would, but it didn't work out.

That's why it's really, really vital that I look fantastic. Because if Brent sees me with —

Oh, thanks, but I guess it's just something you're born with. I mean, I can't really take the credit for having fabulous hair.

Well, sure I take care of it. A girl has to make the best of her assets. Although I know some girls who don't even try. I'll never understand people like that. Especially when someone goes out of their way to help.

You're just trimming the ends, right, Cheryl? I don't want it shorter. I have to look really, really good. I want Brent to spend all night trying to dance with me.

Right, let him eat his heart out. Maybe it'll teach him a lesson.

Eeww, that stuff smells awful. I know, I know. As long as I don't smell when you're finished! Ouch. It's making my eyes tear. Maybe I'd better take my contact lenses out.

Okay.

Doug? Well, Doug's a really nice guy, but I'm not interested in him. I mean, you know, not that way. It was bizarre the way it happened. That's what I started to tell you. I was trying to fix him up with Suzanne Fischetti.

How it started was, I was really, really down because Brent hadn't asked me to this St. Valentine's dance, and whenever I called him he was at soccer practice or something.

So I'm moping around, and Brent isn't calling, even though I'm pretty sure he will, and I'm starting to get really, really depressed. So I turn on the TV and there's this religious show on.

I'm just about to zap it when this woman starts talking about how *she* was really depressed once. Her husband abandoned her, and then she lost her job and she had three kids to feed, and she had to go on welfare.

But then she was watching this very same show, and the minister said, "Are you depressed? Feeling sorry for yourself?" And she sat right up because it was like he was talking straight to her.

And he said that the best way to get over being depressed was to help somebody less fortunate than yourself.

Well, she thought there couldn't be anyone less fortunate than her. But she found soup kitchens and homeless shelters and stuff, and she volunteered a couple of hours a week to work in them.

Ooh — that stings a little. Is it supposed to sting? You don't think I'm allergic to it? I mean, I know I never was before, but I wouldn't want my scalp to break out in a rash and have to shave all my —

Okay. As long as it's supposed to feel like that.

Where was I? Oh, right, soup kitchens and homeless shelters. Anyhow, she said she started to feel better right away. And eventually she got another job and went off welfare and got married again.

But the point was, she didn't sit around feeling sorry for herself, and waiting for something good to happen. She loved her neighbor, and did unto others, and that un-depressed her.

So I got this flash. I mean, like a lightning bolt, or a message from God. I know that sounds corny, but that's how it felt.

This poor woman was just like me. And what was I doing? Sitting around feeling sorry for myself, just like she did.

I thought, there must be lots of people less fortunate than I am. I don't want to sound conceited or anything, but let's face it, I do have a lot going for me. After all, can I help the way I look? Some people are just born attractive.

Well, thanks, Cheryl, but really, the clothes and makeup and all that stuff — it's just a matter of making the most of what you already have. I'm just lucky with what I already have.

So no matter how terrible I felt about Brent and the dance, I knew there were other people with problems even worse than this one little school dance.

Even if it isn't just a *little* dance, but an extremely major highlight of the year that I would

68

kill myself if Brent didn't ask me to.

Anyway, this woman really inspired me, and I thought, Renee, somebody out there needs your help. I mean, a lot of people out there need help. But what could I do? I'm only sixteen, and I'm not really talented at anything.

Okay, I have a sense of style — I really know about clothes. And I'm good with makeup. But what am I going to do? Give dress-for-success lectures at a homeless shelter?

Suzanne Fischetti, the girl I'm telling you about, leads singalongs at the Meadowview Senior Care Home, but she can play the piano. Besides, I knew I couldn't work in an old persons' home because even if there was something useful I could do for them, it would just be so depressing to be around those people.

I can't even watch the TV news when they show nursing home problems. They're so — eeww, you know. Working at Meadowview would just make me more depressed. I had to help people who had problems, but not like problems that were so gruesome that I'd end up even more miserable than I was to begin with.

What kind of curlers are those? They look skinnier than the ones you usually — a spiral perm? What's that? Really? I don't know if I ought to try something new now. Because my hair has to be absolutely perf —

Bounce and spring? Lots of body? Well, my hair has good body, anyway, Cheryl, so — Jody Bannerman? She got one? Well, what do you know? Yeah, she does look great. I hate her, but she looks great. Okay, if you're really, really sure, go ahead.

Where was I? Oh, yeah, helping people. Well, some of the girls in my sorority are volunteers at the county hospital. You know, candy stripers. They have these cute uniforms and help the nurses.

But then I thought, hey, wait a minute. Hospitals are full of sick people.

I know it sounds funny, Cheryl, but think about it a minute. What if I caught something from one of the sick people? And then I couldn't go to the dance because I got sick trying to stop being depressed about not going to the dance? Wouldn't that be totally ironic?

And boom, just at that moment the phone rings and it's Suzanne Fischetti asking what the English assignment was on Friday. Well, she sounds pretty down on herself, and I ask her is anything wrong?

We used to be pretty good friends, but she got really boring and then I joined Gamma Sig and she didn't even want to try for it so we sort of drifted apart.

And she says there's nothing wrong, she just hasn't been feeling too well, but she's going back to school tomorrow and she needs the English assignment.

To tell you the truth, I hadn't even noticed that she was absent, but she just isn't the kind of girl you notice one way of the other. She studies, she works at the old people's home, and she baby-sits. That's her whole life. I mean, she is really dull.

And she doesn't even try to do anything with herself. All right, she hasn't got much to work with, but still, you can always look better if you make an effort.

I ask her if she's going to the dance, and she says no, nobody asked her, and I'm not surprised, because who would? And without even thinking, just to make conversation, I say, if someone did ask you, would you go?

And she says, if the right person did I would.

And I think, hey, beggars can't be choosers, you'd be lucky to go to the dance with *any* person, but I don't say that, of course.

I ask her who the right person is, and she's kind of shy about it, but finally she says, Doug Malloy.

And suddenly, *bam*! It hits me. This is some-one I can help. This is how I can use my talent. I'll take Suzanne under my wing, do a make-over, teach her some basic social skills, and show her how to get Doug interested in her.

I know it won't be easy, but hey — nothing worthwhile is. And I'm not looking for some-thing easy. I'm looking for someone who needs me.

Well, I tell her I bet I can get Doug to ask her to the dance, and she just laughs. And I say, no, really, I can, but you have to put your-self completely in my hands.

And she says, what are you going to do? And I say, come home with me tomorrow after school and I'll show you.

So she laughs again and says, what will you do, give me flirting lessons or something? And I say, well, you can't expect to catch a peacock if you look like a sparrow. Not that Doug's a peacock, but she knows what I mean.

Then there's this long silence and finally she laughs again, but not like she's really amused, and she says, okay, sure, what have I got to lose?

All right, Cheryl. How long do you have to leave it on? I smell like an accident in the chem lab. And these curlers are so *tight*. Okay. Just give me the *Vogue* and *People* and maybe *Elle*. Yeah, if I hold them close enough, I can read without my lenses.

Boy, this is taking a long time. Yeah, I know it always does, but it's just I still have to get shoes. No, I've been looking and looking and I can't find anything. They have to be exactly the right shade and it's too late to get anything dyed. I didn't realize it would be this hard to find them.

Where was I? Oh, right. So the next day, the first thing I do when we get to my house is to analyze Suzanne. You know, critique her good points and her bad points. Of course, there are hardly any good points at all. She's wearing this old plaid shirt and these ratty, rust-colored corduroy pants with an elastic waist-band — I mean, she looks like a lumberjack or something.

Why in the world are you wearing that? I ask her. She looks down at herself and says, what's wrong with what I'm wearing?

And I swear, Cheryl, I'm about to give up on the spot, because I figure this is a hopeless case. But I remember my resolution to help someone, no matter how hard it is.

So I tell her. The colors are totally wrong

for you, your face looks washed out, the pants are sloppy, elastic waistbands are tacky, and why aren't you at least wearing a belt so no one knows that's an elastic waistband?

And haven't you ever heard of blusher? And did you ever tweeze your eyebrows in your *whole life*? They're all over the place like caterpillars.

I mean, I've really got my work cut out for me.

She says, isn't there one thing about me that's not horrible? Well, her hair isn't too bad. You could really do something with it, Cheryl, but I know she can't afford you.

So I say, you have nice hair, and that's really major, but you've got to do something more with it than shampoo it and tie it back with a rubber band.

By the time I finish analyzing her, she's ready to walk out of the house because she realizes what a huge challenge it's going to be to get her in shape. But I tell her, don't be discouraged. I can fix you so you'll look just great, and Doug will ask you to the dance.

I can see she doesn't believe it, she's looking so depressed by this time, and to tell you the truth, I'm not sure I believe it, either. But I'm going to try to make Suzanne happy even if it kills me.

It's going to be fun, I tell her. You'll see.

But I'm thinking, where do I *start*? Finally, I grab a pair of tweezers. I figure she'll see a dramatic change right away, and I can't work on her clothes until I go through her closet, so we'll do the eyebrows and makeup today and work on the clothes tomorrow.

So I start plucking her eyebrows and she starts yelling and screaming. "Hey, this isn't fun!" And I tell her what you always tell me, how you have to suffer for beauty sometimes. And believe me, Cheryl, the way she looks, she never spent a second suffering.

But when I'm finished and she checks in the mirror, she says, hey, they're nice! Sure they're nice, I tell her. Now that you don't have two caterpillars over your eyes, they give your face some definition. It's not such a blob.

Then I show her how to apply mascara and blusher and all, and when we're finished with the makeup, she can't stop staring at herself in the mirror. She can't believe the difference.

And neither can I. You see, I tell her, even you can look decent if you make the effort.

She says, oh, thanks, Renee — a little sarcastically — but I know she's really grateful because she's still staring at the mirror like she doesn't recognize herself.

Then I give her a whole bunch of makeup that I don't use anymore. I mean, she doesn't have *anything*, so even if the colors aren't exactly perfect for her, they're better than nothing. I tell her to practice at home with her eyes and the blusher and stuff like I showed her.

The next day we go to her house to do her clothes.

Well, to make a long story short, I want to burn almost everything she owns. I manage to put three outfits together that are not totally disgusting, and I talk about accessorizing and how to do a lot with a little. But this is like trying to make a Chanel purse out of a Hefty Bag.

I drag her to the mall — and I mean, I really have to drag her. She's whining about some math test she has to study for, and how she doesn't have time to shop. But I am not about to listen to that nonsense.

I try to teach her everything I ever learned about clothes in two hours. The only problem is, she's got a total of thirty-seven dollars to spend. She buys one sweater. On sale.

Back to my house. I go through the guest

room closet to find some of my old stuff to give her. I mean, even my mistakes are an improvement over her clothes.

But we're not the same size, she says. I'm four inches taller than you. And thinner. That's what safety pins are for, I tell her. And you can wear boots with the pants that are too short. You're still going to look better in my clothes than in the stuff you wear.

And it's true. She tries on a few things — okay, maybe they're not the height of fashion, but they're a hundred thousand times better than what she usually wears.

I send her home with four outfits, all labeled so she knows what goes with what. Now she's got seven days of clothes, which gives her seven days to look her best — at least, as good as she can look — which should be enough time to get Doug interested in her and ask her to the dance.

The next day I start teaching her how to act with boys. If I thought making her look good was a challenge, getting her to loosen up and act feminine was totally impossible. You'd think I was asking her to throw herself under a train.

I can't walk like that! she says. It looks like I'm trying to imitate Marilyn Monroe.

Well, I shot back, the way you walk now you look like the Hunchback of Notre Dame. I just want you to stop slumping over and walk with one foot straight in front of the other, like the models do. That way you have a nice, natural sway in your hips.

But it's not natural for *me*, she says. It looks phony and artificial. Maybe so, I say, but how far have you gotten staying pure and natural? Nowhere, that's how far.

Then I try to teach her how to look at a boy. You know, from under her eyelashes — which, by the way, are nice and long now that she's learned how to use mascara. And she says, oh, come on. That stuff went out with Scarlett O'Hara.

And Scarlett O'Hara went out with a hundred guys a month, I tell her. I don't notice you going out with one guy a *year*.

Which shuts her up. But I'm getting nowhere. I decide what she needs is a live demonstration to see how to do all this stuff, and to see that it really works.

The next day at lunch we go into the cafeteria, and I spot Doug on the lunch line. Perfect, I say. Now we put into action what I've been trying to teach you.

I can't, she says, and sort of shrinks back and

shakes her head. Yes, you can, I say, and drag her over to Doug.

But she's right. She can't. She just stands there, hunched over as usual, and barely mumbles hello to him when he notices us.

So I start the demonstration. I ask Doug to let us get in line in front of him and I start chatting with him. I sort of lean against the railing, you know, stretching a little, and when he talks I look up at him like he's the most fascinating person in the whole world.

So naturally he follows us to a table. As we're sitting down I whisper to Suzanne, now's your chance. *You* start talking to him.

But she freezes. She doesn't say a word. She doesn't look at him. She does absolutely nothing but stare down at her tray and poke at her food.

It's hopeless. What can I do? I'd planned to sit there and just blend into the woodwork while she turned the charm on Doug, but she doesn't have any charm to turn on. If I don't say something we'll sit through the whole lunch in total silence.

So I start talking to him and he starts talking back. And I thought, Suzanne is right. He really is a nice guy. Which I tell her after lunch.

But she's so miserable, she probably didn't

hear me. I guess she was feeling kind of dumb for being too shy to even try and get Doug to notice her. I mean, here I go to all that trouble getting her looking decent, and trying to teach her to act the teeniest bit sexy and self-confident, and she just sits there like a lump. As if she'd learned absolutely nothing in the last three days.

I couldn't blame her for feeling dumb, but I was also pretty irritated. When you set out to help somebody, it's kind of disappointing to see them bomb like that.

But I try to sound reassuring. Tomorrow's another day, and I'll give her some more tips on how to talk and act, and she'll have more self-confidence and soon she'll be able to talk to Doug almost as easily as I can.

Though I don't really believe it.

Finally! I thought you'd never wash this stuff out. We're almost finished, aren't we? Whew, good.

Yeah, the water's just right. No, it's not too hot.

Anyway, she doesn't come home with me that afternoon. She says she did lousy on the math test and Mr. Alvarez is going to let her take a makeup, so she has to spend the afternoon studying.

I say, Suzanne, the dance is eight days away, you don't have that much time left. But my makeup test is tomorrow, she says.

Suzanne, I say, where are your priorities? You've got the whole rest of the year to pull up your math grade, but only a few days to get Doug to ask you to the dance.

Could I have an extra towel, Cheryl? Yeah, it's a good thing I took them out. I think I got some of that stuff in my eye. There's water down my back, too. Ick.

Anyway, Suzanne won't budge. So what can I do? I tried to help her, I've been killing myself trying to help her, and what's she doing to help herself? Nothing. If she was really interested in Doug she wouldn't make such a big deal about having to study.

Well, the next day Doug starts talking to me at lunch, and walks me to my next class. And when the class is over, he's waiting for me outside.

Yay! Just the blow-drying and styling left. I can't wait to see how I look. Although I'm beginning to wonder if I should have tried something different right before a major, major event like —

Yes, that's true. If I was afraid to try new things, I'd look as blah as Suzanne.

Okay. So Doug is waiting for me everywhere. But every time he speaks to me, I *swear* I talk about Suzanne. I'm still trying to help her even though she won't —

Louder? Okay. Can you hear me now? Yeah, it's hard over the blow-dryer. So I'm really talking up Suzanne, and trying to keep his mind on her, but it's totally obvious that he's not interested in Suzanne. He can't keep his mind off *me*.

Now, here it is, one week to the dance, and I've turned down two other guys because I'm so sure Brent *has* to ask me, but Brent hasn't asked me. Then — are you ready? — Suzanne tells me that Brent asked *Jody Bannerman* to the dance. That's right. The very same.

Well, I can't believe it. I'm totally destroyed, totally in despair. But Suzanne? Well, you'd think she'd show a little compassion after all I've tried to do for her. You know what she says? She says, that's too bad. You must be pretty disappointed.

Too bad? Pretty disappointed? Like, that's all she can say? That's all the sympathy she can manage? I suddenly realize this is a girl who absolutely doesn't understand the first thing about deep feelings and real emotions and the kind of suffering the human heart can experience.

And that afternoon Doug says, I know it's kind of short notice, and I'm sure you've already got a date. I mean, a girl like you is not sitting around waiting for the phone to ring. But if you by any chance haven't accepted anyone yet, would you go to the Valentine's dance with me?

I don't answer him right away, because I really never would have looked at him twice except for Suzanne's sake. But whether I go with him or not, he's definitely not going to ask Suzanne, so how would it help her if I refused?

But there is this ethical question. Like, it was Suzanne who wanted him, and I don't really care about him that much. But on the other hand, I *have* to go to that dance, and Brent has to see me there. I tried and tried to help Suzanne, but where did it get me? Or her?

In fact, I probably spent so much time concentrating on fixing her up, and getting her a date, that I wasted valuable time I could have been using to work on Brent.

And for nothing. She turned out to be hopeless.

So I said, sure I'll go to the dance with you. Well, you should have seen the look on his face. Like he'd just won the lottery, or something. I figured, at least I made one person happy. Even though it wasn't the person I set out to make happy.

I did my best for Suzanne, I really did. I mean, how much more could I have done? I guess there are some people who just don't want to be helped.

Ooh, at last! I can't wait to see it. Let me get my lenses in.

There. Okay, here we go!

Oh, my God! Cheryl, *what have you done to my hair?*

DON'T LET THE
BEDBUGS BITE

I admit that when my mother told me she was going to marry Tina Grossman's father, I did not take the news very well.

"You can't do this to me!"

"I'm not doing anything to you, Sally," my mother said. "I'm marrying a very nice man whom I love very much."

"And making Gruesome Grossman my sister! You know how many times she beat me up?"

"She never beat you up."

"Well, she threatened to. Twice a week. For three years."

"Sally, that was in fifth grade."

"And sixth grade," I said, "and seventh grade."

"She had problems," my mother admitted. "How would you feel if your mother left you to run off with a vacuum-cleaner salesman?"

"No worse than I feel now," I retorted. "At least I wouldn't have to worry about my stepsister murdering me in my sleep."

Gruesome Grossman, my stepsister. The thought was too horrible to contemplate. Sure, I knew my mother had been going out with Tina's father for a year. But they'd been trying to keep it a secret because they both teach at Locksley Hall High. My school.

My mother had sworn me to secrecy, and even though I was dying to tell my friends that she was dating their German teacher, I didn't. Even when my best friend, Selena, got a massive crush on him and wrote him thirty-seven love notes that she (fortunately) never mailed.

They didn't want to be teased and spied on. They didn't want to be the object of sordid teenage gossip and evil rumors. I could understand that. After all, I'm a teenager. I love sordid gossip and evil rumors.

But marriage? They were two middle-aged teachers with practically grown daughters. Why did they have to get married? Why couldn't they just go right on sneaking around, without forcing their children into this bizarre parody of a family?

I dropped into the nearest chair and glared at my mother. "Does Tina know about the impending nuptials?" I said "nuptials" with such disgust that my mother winced.

"No. Remember, she was in my history class when I started seeing Don. And then, when I had to flunk her, we thought . . ."

"See! Even her father's afraid of her. And she must *hate* you. Can't you tell this is never going to work?"

"It will work," my mother said firmly, "if we work at making it work."

I scowled at her. "Nobody could work that hard."

It's not that I resented my mother remarrying. I wasn't jealous about "sharing" her with someone else. In fact, for years after my father died, I tried to fix her up with men so I could have a daddy again.

The man who came to service the oil burner, the shoe salesman who fitted me at Wee Walk Inn, even the UPS driver who occasionally delivered a package to our house — I considered all of them potential father material.

Of course, I was eight years old at the time,

and kept seeing all these old movies on TV where a little kid brings two people together who never realize they love each other until they both realize they love *her*.

But the little kid never ended up with a stepsister. Let alone a stepsister like Tina Grossman.

It was about this time that Tina — the Terror of Tyler Elementary School — began terrorizing me. Oh, she picked on other kids, too. I wasn't the only one who was afraid of her. But maybe I was the one who was most afraid of her. So naturally I was the kid she most enjoyed bullying.

I handed over lunch money, granola bars, homework, snap bracelets — even pencils with my name printed on them that my grandmother had given me for Christmas.

All she had to do was stand over me with her fists on her hips and say, "Gimme that!" At first I'd say no. Then she'd say, "Gimme that or I'll break your arm."

I generally decided that I needed my arm more than the lunch money, granola bar, or whatever it was she was trying to extort from me that day.

Maybe that's why I longed for a father so

much. Maybe I thought he'd protect me from Tina. But I'd gotten over it. And eventually, Tina got tired of terrorizing me, and channeled her aggression into school sports, where she became the captain of the softball team, the volleyball team, and the basketball team. Possibly by threatening to break all the other players' arms if they didn't elect her captain.

Well, I was finally getting a father. Who was just as afraid of Tina as everyone else.

"When's the wedding?" I asked sourly. "And is there time to enroll me in boarding school before then?"

"July," my mother said.

"July?" I groaned. "That's only two months away. It's hardly enough time to write my will."

"I know it seems soon," my mother said. "That's why Don and I thought you girls ought to get better acquainted before then."

"We could hardly be worse acquainted," I said before I realized what she was getting at.

"So Saturday we're all going into the city together," she went on. "We have marvelous plans. First we'll go to a Yankee game."

"I hate baseball," I said.

"Then on to a nice restaurant for dinner," she continued.

"I'm on a diet."

"And after dinner we have tickets for *Oui, Oui, Odette*."

That shut me up. Momentarily. *Oui, Oui, Odette* was the hottest musical on Broadway.

"And then Tina will come back here to sleep over." She said it rapidly, as if hoping she could slip it by me. Unfortunately, I heard it.

"It will be a wonderful day," she promised.

"It will be a day that will live in infamy," I replied.

When Mr. Grossman came to pick us up Saturday morning, Tina was sullen and withdrawn. Obviously her father had told her about the wedding plans. Obviously she was as thrilled as I was about the prospect of joining our families.

She was wearing a white sleeveless T-shirt that displayed her overdeveloped biceps, and a denim skirt. For Tina this was practically formal wear. I couldn't remember ever seeing her in a skirt before.

She'd even tried to tame her long, frizzy black hair with gel or something. It wasn't as wild as it usually looked.

Tina and I immediately positioned ourselves as far apart as possible in the backseat of her father's car. She stared out the left window, silent. I stared out the right window. Silent.

My mother and Tina's father tried to get a conversation going.

"Beautiful weather for the ball game, isn't it?" he said.

"If you like baseball," I said.

"Tina loves baseball, don't you, Tina?" my mother said. "Your dad says you're a real Yankee fan."

"Yeah," said Tina.

Things went on like this until I actually began to feel a little guilty about not trying to be nice. I liked Mr. Grossman — whom I'd been calling Don for three months. I supposed it wasn't entirely his fault that Tina was such a creep.

So as we approached the Midtown Tunnel I admired the city skyline. "There's the Chrysler Building," I said. Its golden roof and spire gleamed in the sun. "Isn't it beautiful?" Just trying to be pleasant.

"Yeah," said Tina.

"It's my favorite building in New York," I said. "What's your favorite building?"

Finally she turned away from the window. She looked at me as if she thought I was nuts. "Favorite *building*?" She curled her lip in contempt.

I heard a sigh from the driver's seat.

We drove the rest of the way to Yankee Stadium without anybody trying to be nice to anybody else.

But once in our seats, Tina began to show signs of life. Too much life, if you ask me. She cheered or groaned with every pitch. She leaped up at every crack of the bat. She screamed extremely foul things to the umpires, to the Red Sox, to the hot-dog vendor who blocked her view, and to the Yankee batter who failed to hit with three men on base in the bottom of the last inning.

I was practically deaf by the time the game ended, and secretly thrilled that the Yankees had lost. Anything that made Tina so miserable made me happy.

Tina sulked all the way through dinner. We ate at a very classy, very expensive restaurant called Chez Philippe. I loved my lobster bisque, my rack of lamb, and the three pastries I selected from the extravagant dessert cart.

Our parents were really blowing a bundle on this stepsister-bonding business.

Tina had a hamburger. And ice cream.

The only way the two of us would ever bond would be if someone Krazy-Glued our shoulders together.

I think we were all pretty tired when we headed for the theater. The strain of trying to act like one big happy family was wearing us down.

Although Tina couldn't have been particularly worn down, since she wasn't trying at all.

And much as I wanted to see *Oui, Oui, Odette*, I knew that the minute it ended, I'd have to go home with Tina. A grim, ugly prospect that took the edge off my anticipation of the show.

But once *Oui, Oui, Odette* started, I forgot everything — my wicked stepsister-to-be, Don, the boring ball game, all the French pastry I was digesting. The show was a takeoff on 1930s musicals. There was terrific tap-dancing, bouncy songs, and great costumes. I was so immersed in the whole experience that I didn't even move from my seat during intermission. I just waited impatiently for the next act to start, not wanting to break the mood the play had created.

At the curtain calls, I applauded so long and so hard that my hands began to sting. I glanced over at Tina. To my surprise, she was clapping as enthusiastically as I was.

"Wasn't that a great show?" I said as we walked to the parking garage.

"Yeah," Tina agreed. "It was." I was surprised that she added two more words than was absolutely necessary to reply.

I began to hum the tune to "Tap, *Tout le Monde*, Tap," the show's big production number. I was even more surprised when Tina started humming along with me.

But once in the car, she reverted to type. She sat all the way over on the other side of the seat again, and leaned her head against the window.

Don and my mother kept up an enthusiastic stream of chatter about what a wonderful day it had been.

I still had to get through the night.

I tried to tell myself that it was, after all, only one night — eight hours. We were both tired and would probably go right to sleep.

But of course, it wasn't only one night. It was the first night of the rest of my life. Or at least until I went to college. And although it seemed unlikely now that she would murder me in my sleep, what about having to deal with her the rest of the time? What about breakfasts and dinners and summers and trips and — *everything*?

I felt a very unpleasant tightness in my

stomach — and it wasn't because of the three desserts.

There was a soft rumble from Tina's direction. I looked over at her. She was slumped against the window, snoring. Even sound asleep she looked tough.

When we got back to our house, Don declared that the day had been a rousing success.

"You girls ought to get right to bed," my mother urged. "Sally will show you where everything is, Tina."

Don hugged Tina and said he'd be back to pick her up in the morning, Tina got her sleeping bag and followed me up the stairs.

I felt like I was walking the Last Mile.

"The bathroom's there." I pointed. "You can use it first. My room's there."

"I don't see why we have to sleep in the same room," she said. Except for *Oui, Oui, Odette*, it was the only thing we agreed on all day. "I can put my sleeping bag anywhere."

"I don't see why, either," I said. "It's not like we're going to magically become friends overnight." Or ever. I was too tired to worry about insulting her. And she was probably too tired to punch me.

I got into my pajamas while she used the

bathroom. She came back into my room wearing a green football jersey nightshirt, and unrolled her sleeping bag near my closet.

I spent a long time in the bathroom. I washed my face for five minutes and brushed my teeth till my gums nearly bled, hoping she'd be asleep by the time I got back to my room.

But she wasn't. She was lying in her sleeping bag, arms behind her head, staring at the ceiling.

"Well, good night," I said.

I climbed into bed and switched off the lamp on my night table. I punched my pillow a few times, pulled the sheet halfway up over my head, and scrunched around under the covers until I was comfortable. Or as comfortable as I could get with Gruesome Grossman sharing my room.

"Uh — Sally?"

I was startled. It was the first time she'd called me by name all day.

I pulled the sheet down from my nose. "What is it?"

"Sometimes I don't sleep too well away from home." Her voice was soft, tentative — almost childlike.

I didn't know what to say. I didn't know what she was getting at. Was there something I was supposed to do to help her sleep? And why did she sound so meek?

"I sometimes have trouble sleeping in a strange bed, too," I said. "Not that you're in a bed, but — "

"Your room is so dark," she said.

"It's nighttime," I reminded her. "It's supposed to be dark."

"My room isn't this dark."

"What, you sleep with a nightlight or something?" I blurted it out without realizing how insulting it sounded.

There was a long silence. Long enough for me to figure out that I'd stumbled onto the truth. Gruesome Grossman slept with a nightlight. Gruesome Grossman was afraid of the dark.

The shock was enough to get the adrenaline pumping through my system. Suddenly I wasn't sleepy anymore. I sat up and flicked on the lamp.

Tina was hunched up like a snail in her sleeping bag. I looked at her for a long time before speaking.

"I didn't think," I said finally, "that you were afraid of *anything*."

"I'm not afraid," she snapped. "I just don't like it too dark."

"Listen, everyone's afraid of *something*," I said. I nearly added, "I'm afraid of you." But I didn't.

"I'm not afraid of the dark," she insisted. She sounded like herself again. Gruesome Grossman, spoiling for a fight, ready to deck anyone who disagreed with her.

"Okay, okay," I said. Not because I was afraid she'd deck me. But because I knew she must be feeling pretty embarrassed about this. And I found, to my surprise, that I had no desire to make her feel worse.

"Do you want me to leave the lamp on?" I asked.

She hesitated again. "But then you won't be able to sleep."

"Well," I agreed, "I do like it pretty dark." I thought for a moment. "I have an idea. There's a bulb in my closet."

I got out of bed and opened the closet door. The light came on. I closed the door halfway and got back into bed. I turned off the lamp.

"How's that?" I asked.

A narrow shaft of light illuminated the area around Tina's sleeping bag. If I turned toward the window and pulled the covers up to my nose again, it would hardly bother me.

"That's good," Tina said. She sounded relieved, as if she'd made it through a horror movie without having a heart attack.

"Thanks," she added.

"No problem," I said. "Good night."

She yawned deeply. "Good night," she said. "Sleep tight. Don't let the bedbugs bite."

TEACHER FROM THE PREHISTORIC PLANET

William Fraser, teacher of American History at John Jay High School, looked out at the thirty-five youthful faces in his first-period class.

It was the first day of the new school year. Mr. Fraser, fighting his habitual pessimism, gave himself the inner pep talk he used to psych himself up at the beginning of every year.

If I can reach just one or two of them . . . if I can get just a few kids turned on to how exciting history can be . . . to the drama of the American experience . . . If one kid would ask me a question without wanting to know if it will be on the final — would that make it all worthwhile?

Maybe, he answered himself. If they doubled my salary, too.

Benny LaMotta sprawled in his seat, miserably trying to figure out a way to switch classes. Ferret-Face Fraser was his worst nightmare — everyone's worst nightmare, not just Benny's.

Sour, sarcastic, demanding, loading you down with homework, handing out D's and F's like he had a quota to fill before the marking period ended.

Toughest teacher in the whole school. I don't need this aggravation, Benny thought. Why couldn't I have gotten Ms. Steinfeld? Nice, sympathetic, easy marker. Easy on the eyes, too. I'd pay attention in *her* class. Might even learn something.

Why's he looking at me like that? He hates me already. I can tell. And I haven't even done anything.

I'll bet he remembers my brother.

I've got to get out of this class. *Today*.

"Benjamin LaMotta? . . . Benjamin LaMotta? . . . *Mr. LaMotta!*"

"Huh? You calling me?"

"We're taking the roll, Mr. LaMotta. If it's

not asking too much, would you please respond when I call your name?"

"I didn't hear you."

"I hope you'll pay more attention when it's time to learn something. You're not, by any chance, related to Sal LaMotta?"

"He's my brother."

I could resign right now, William Fraser said to himself, pen poised over his roll book. I could just walk out of this classroom, into the parking lot, start my car, and take off for Montana. I don't suppose many men my age become cowboys, but I enjoyed *City Slickers*, and it's probably a clean, healthy life. All that fresh air, and the mountains, and no sixteen-year-old kids.

He remembered Sal LaMotta very well. He wondered if he were on Death Row yet.

I knew it, Benny told himself. Hates me already, just because of Sal. It doesn't matter how hard I work, he'd still flunk me. I might as well not even try. What'll I do if I can't get Ms. Steinfeld? End up in summer school, that's what I'll do.

* * *

I'm jumping to conclusions, Mr. Fraser thought. Just because his brother was a problem doesn't mean he will be. All right, so he's trying to gouge out the arm of his desk with a Swiss Army knife. That doesn't make him a bad person. Maybe he's bored.

"Mr. LaMotta. Weapons are not allowed in the classroom."

"Weapons? What weapons?"

"The knife, Mr. LaMotta. I won't take it away from you this time, but I don't want to see it in here again."

"This isn't a weapon. It's a Swiss Army knife."

"The Swiss Army will be surprised to learn that their knife isn't a weapon." Well, a laugh. Not from Benny, of course. Maybe the joke is too sophisticated for him.

"I'm just trying to scrape the gum off. Every time I put my arm there, it sticks to it."

"Then don't put your arm there." Another laugh. What an audience. These kids are so bored, they'll laugh at anything. Or maybe they're just grateful I haven't started teaching yet.

In the class five minutes and he's pulling the sarcasm on me. Sure, pick on LaMotta. Make fun of LaMotta. Single out LaMotta. You don't know *anyone* yet, but you know you hate me.

Well, I hate you, too. You're as much of a crud as everyone says you are. And I'd call you something worse, except you can probably read my mind.

Yeah. You're probably some kind of mutant. Ferret-Face Fraser, the Mutant from Mars. Ha! Let me write that down and shoot it over to Charlie. He'll love it.

Yes, Mr. LaMotta, I saw you write the note. I saw you fold it into a paper glider and throw it two rows over. Even you couldn't be so stupid as to think I wouldn't see that.

You want me to tell you to bring it up front. You want me to tell you to read it out loud. I'm not going to fall for it. After fifteen years of teaching, I'm too smart to ask someone to read a note before I know what's in it.

No doubt it will be something embarrassing. Some comment on my physical appearance, or my manhood, or my parentage. Oh, no, kiddo. I'm not falling for it.

Whoops. Missed Charlie completely. Oh, great, Tiffany Watts got it. Geez, what a look.

Well, *excuuuse* me, Miss Prissy Face. I didn't write it about you, did I?

Why don't you show it to him? That's just your style. Never too early to start sucking up to the teacher.

I don't care. I hope he reads it. I know how he feels about me. Let him see the feeling is mutual.

Four years of college, Mr. Fraser thought, two years of postgraduate work, for what? To stand up here and make sure kids don't throw paper airplanes or chop up their desks. I should have joined the police force. I'd make ten thousand more a year and get to carry a gun.

"All right, everyone, we're using new books this year, so if you've borrowed test answers and term papers from last year's students, they aren't going to do you any good."

Another laugh. I'm on a roll.

"Some of my reading assignments may sound long, but as you can see, there are plenty of illustrations in the text. Some of them even take up the whole page. We're going to start out in sixteen-twenty — "

Benny LaMotta didn't hear him. Didn't notice that Mr. Fraser was making jokes. He was busy imagining a biography for him.

He's not from Mars, thought Benny. He's from some planet where they haven't evolved yet. Where they're old and fossilized and their blood is getting thin and the prehistoric animals are beginning to be smarter than the people. Yeah, like the people are all Neanderthals, really primitive, and Ferret-Face is one of the last remaining survivors, and that's why he came here. They need fresh, young blood, and every year a few students disappear, because Ferret-Face kidnaps them and —

Hey, this is pretty good. Maybe I ought to write it down.

The planet Crapton was dying. The sun hardly ever shone there anymore. The few remaining survivors were dried-up old fossils. All the young people had died of boredom. Mainly because of the most evil, the most boring Craptonian of them all.

His name was Fraser . . .

Is he actually taking notes? Only three people in the room are taking notes, and he's one of them? Maybe I misjudged him. Look at him scribbling away. Well, I guess you really can't tell a book by its cover. Or a student by his brother.

Was that the bell? Benny looked up from his notebook. He'd written four pages without realizing it. Time sure flies, he thought, when you're trashing someone.

". . . and I couldn't help noticing that — *keep your seats, please*. I'm still speaking." Even though no one is listening. "I couldn't help noticing that a few students have gotten off to a promising start. While most of you were staring out the window or contemplating lunch or wondering how the Mets are doing, some members of this class were actually paying attention. Like Mr. LaMotta."

"Huh?" Benny looked up, startled. Why did everyone laugh? he wondered. Had he said something funny?

"I'm pleased to see you using a ballpoint instead of a knife," Mr. Fraser said. "The pen is mightier than the sword, after all." I can't believe I said something that trite. I'm trying to encourage him, and I sound like a stuffy old fossil.

"At least you'll be ready for the quiz to-morrow."

They're screaming. They're howling. They look like a pack of mad dogs. A quiz on the second day of school.

"Yes, a quiz. Stop whining. On the work we covered today and on pages thirteen to thirty-two in your text." At least this way I have a chance of scaring them into doing the assignment. They certainly won't do it because they're interested in history.

A quiz? Tomorrow? He's got to be kidding. Benny stood up lazily, ignoring the racket created by thirty-four indignant kids stomping out of the room.

He didn't know what Ferret-Face had meant by the notes he was supposed to be taking, but he knew he wasn't reading any twenty pages and studying for a test the first day of school.

No sir. No way. He was heading right down to his guidance counselor to get his class changed.

"Benjamin? May I see you for a moment before you leave?"

Benny pointed at himself. "Me?" Mr. Fraser nodded encouragingly.

Benny couldn't help feeling suspicious. He approached the teacher slowly, like a boxer sizing up his opponent at the beginning of the first round. But Ferret-Face was smiling.

"I think we may have gotten off on the wrong foot," he said.

"Oh, that's okay," said Benny. It didn't matter which foot they'd gotten off on. He wasn't going to be here long.

"No it's not," Mr. Fraser said. "I'm afraid that my experience with your brother influenced my expectations of you."

"Yeah, I figured," said Benny. "I get that a lot."

"I suppose you do. It's not really fair. Where is your brother now, by the way?"

"In Indiana."

Strange, thought Mr. Fraser. I don't remember hearing about a crime wave in Indiana. "What's he doing?"

"He works for a newspaper."

"Delivering it?"

"No," said Benny. "He's a sports columnist. And he's writing a book."

"Writing a book?" William Fraser suddenly felt as if the room were spinning. Sal LaMotta writing a book?

"Well, I gotta go," Benny said. "Gotta see my guidance counselor."

"Just one more thing," Mr. Fraser said. "I wanted to tell you that I was pleased to see you taking my class so seriously. I just didn't — expect it. Especially since I'm afraid I indulged in some sarcasm at your expense."

"Hey, it's okay," Benny answered. "I'm not going to be staying in this class anyhow."

"What do you mean?"

"I — uh — I've got to get my schedule changed. Because of a — um — conflict. I have to switch to Ms. Steinfeld's class. I have a free period now, so — "

"I'm afraid that won't be possible, Benny. You'll have to resolve your scheduling conflict some other way."

"What?" Benny felt a wave of nausea overcome him. "Why won't it be possible?"

"Ms. Steinfeld isn't teaching American History this year."

"Not? Ms. Steinfeld teaching? American?" The words came out crazily, but Mr. Fraser understood them.

He shook his head. "I'm afraid you're stuck with me. But you're off to a great start. That's why I asked to speak to you."

"Me? Speak? Why?"

"Those notes you were taking so conscientiously," Mr. Fraser said. "I'd like to read them."

"Notes? The notes? Taking? In my notebook — those notes?" Benny clutched the notebook to his chest.

"I really want to see what you got out of my class," Mr. Fraser said. "It's helpful for a teacher to know what parts of a lesson make the most impression."

He plucked the notebook away from Benny's chest and slid it into his desk drawer.

"No!" Benny gasped. He felt as if he were choking. "I — I have to — my next class. Need it for my next class."

"But you have a free period now," Mr. Fraser reminded him. "Look, I'll tell you what. I can read the notes while my next class is coming in. You come back at the end of this period and I'll return them."

Benny felt the room begin to sway. This couldn't be happening. Wasn't there some kind of law against a teacher snatching a student's private notebook?

"My handwriting," he said desperately. "You can't read — bad penmanship — "

Mr. Fraser laughed. "After all these years

of teaching, I can read anybody's handwriting."

"But I — but I — " Think I'm going to faint. Benny's life, short as it was, passed before his eyes.

"Now, Benny, come on." Mr. Fraser patted him on the shoulder. "I don't care what your handwriting looks like." He smiled a warm, heartening, optimistic smile.

"It's what you have to say that counts."

BEWARE THE IDES
OF NOVEMBER

"A red-letter day! All the signs are in your favor! Take advantage of the many wonderful opportunities that come your way!"

That's what my horoscope said for Thursday, November 12th.

And it wasn't one of those one-size-fits-all horoscopes that run in the daily newspapers. This was a personalized astrological forecast prepared *"Especially for you, NIKKI FELD-MAN!"* by famed astrologer and psychic Stella Amarillo.

"She's uncanny," my friend Bess had raved. "Almost everything she predicted for me came true. Just try it for a month. It only costs nine ninety-five."

Well, it was November, and the weather was bleak and raw and rainy, and I was going through one of those dismal periods when my spirit felt as dreary as the weather.

Anything, I thought, to break the tedium. So I sent Stella Amarillo $9.95 (plus postage and handling) and received my Monthly Forecast and Predictions on November 9th.

I was pretty impressed for the first two days. For the 10th my horoscope said, "Be careful of what you wish for today. It might come true."

I spent the whole morning wishing I didn't have to take the biology test seventh period, because I had spent all of last evening reading the stuff Stella Amarillo had sent.

And right after lunch I had to race out of English to the girls' room, where I spent fifteen minutes throwing up. The nurse said there was a virus going around, but I was sure it was the cafeteria's meat loaf.

Whatever it was, I spent the rest of the afternoon on a cot in the health office, and didn't have to take the biology test.

So I got what I wished for, but it wasn't pleasant.

Then on Wednesday my forecast said, "Financial concerns are foremost in your mind today." As it turned out, I'd forgotten my wallet and didn't have any lunch money. (Which may have saved me from another case of food poisoning, come to think of it.)

Not exactly earth-shattering predictions, but close enough for Bess to say, "See? I told you she was incredible!"

Then came November 12th, my "red-letter day," the day of wonderful opportunities, the day all the signs were supposed to be in my favor.

From the time I left the house that morning, every sign I ran into read: DANGER, SLIPPERY WHEN WET! BEWARE OF DOG! DON'T EVEN THINK OF PARKING HERE!!

The first wonderful opportunity came my way on the school bus. There was an empty seat. Unfortunately, it was next to Duane Bellinger. I hesitated because Duane Bellinger is a very unappealing person, who for some mysterious reason, seems to like me.

"Hey, Feldman, move it!" Robby Randazzo pushed me forward. I remembered Stella Amarillo's advice. Take advantage of every opportunity. Sitting down was better than standing up, right?

Wrong.

Robby shoved me into the seat. I landed —

heavily — on Duane's lunch bag. I felt the squoosh and jumped up. Duane grabbed the bag, Robby Randazzo laughed uproariously, and I felt something damp and slimy on the seat of my jeans.

"What *is* that?" I screeched. I jumped up and craned my neck around, trying to see my rear end.

"My jelly sandwich," Duane said apologetically. "Open-faced. I'm trying to drop a few pounds."

"Aw, no!" I moaned. "Is that grape? It's all over my pants!"

Duane handed me a napkin. Robby offered to help me wipe off the jelly.

I dabbed futilely at my jeans. "What kind of a diet are you on?" I growled at Duane. "You put a quart of jelly on a piece of bread and you leave the top off to save calories?"

He looked miserable. I didn't know which bothered him more — that he'd ruined my jeans or that I'd ruined his lunch.

I headed for the girls' room the minute I got into school. I washed out as much of the grape jelly as I could in the sink, and held my pants up to the hand blower to dry.

It took forever. And when the jeans were dry, instead of a wet, gooey purple stain, I was left with a dry, stiff purple stain. And was ten minutes late to math class. So that everyone could see me walk to my seat in the last row with a purple splotch on my backside.

But in gym class, things began to look up. We were playing basketball, and I was still so angry at Duane and Robby Randazzo that I channeled all my hostility into the game.

I scored three baskets, two foul shots, and stole the ball twice. Ms. Carlton was very impressed.

"Fantastic, Nikki! You really played above yourself today."

"It's a good way to blow off steam," I panted.

"That's what I keep trying to tell you girls," she agreed. "If you can play like that consistently, you ought to try out for the team."

"I don't think so," I said. "I haven't usually got this much steam to blow off."

I don't always shower after gym, but this time I needed to. I washed up quickly and towel-dried my hair. I had a history test next period, which I would have enough trouble with even if I started on time.

Shelby Gutierrez lent me her dryer so I could do a fast blow out, just enough to look semi-decent. I plugged it into a socket next to the mirror, flicked it on, and all the lights in the bathroom went out.

"Nikki! What did you do to my dryer?" Shelby pulled it away from me. "You broke it."

"She didn't break your dryer," someone else said. "She shorted out the locker room. Everything's dark."

"What makes you think it's my fault?" I asked irritably. "Maybe there's an outage in the whole building."

There was. But it didn't last long. Just long enough so that all I could do with my wet hair was to drag a comb through it and let it hang.

Just long enough for me to have to dress in near darkness, so that I didn't see that I had closed my locker door on the loose end of one thread — *one thread* — of my yellow Shaker-knit sweater.

Just long enough to be out of the locker room and halfway up the stairs before Bess said, "Nikki, do you know your sweater's coming apart in the back?"

"What are you talking — "

I felt her finger run down my bare spine. "It's completely separated," she said.

"What? How could — "

The lights flickered on again.

"Look at that," she said. "You've got a thread loose. It's stretched all the way back to — "

"No," I moaned. "Oh, please, *no*." I twisted around. Sure enough, a strand of cotton trailed behind me. My sweater was divided halfway up my back, exposing quite a few inches of skin, and the clasp of my bra.

I slumped against the banister. "What am I going to do?" I wailed.

"Well," Bess began, "if you want to save the sweater, you'd better follow the thread back to the locker room."

"I mean now! For the rest of the day! I can't go around like *this*."

"Do you have an extra shirt or anything down here?" she asked.

"Only my gym shirt."

"I guess you'd better wear it."

"I can't wear that! It's all sweaty."

"All right, calm down," she said. "I'll go upstairs to your locker and get your jacket. Do you think it's long enough to cover that stain on your jeans?"

"If it was long enough to cover the stain on my jeans," I shrieked, "I wouldn't *have* a stain on my jeans! I'd have a stain on my jacket!"

She bolted up the stairs as if she wanted to

get away from me as fast as possible.

And who wouldn't? I was a walking disaster zone. If one more "wonderful opportunity" came my way, I'd wrap that loose thread around my neck and hang myself.

I sighed pitifully and twisted the cotton strand around my finger. I wanted to break off the thread before the whole sweater unraveled. But the cotton was too strong. No matter how hard I tried, I couldn't break it.

There was only one thing to do. I started back toward the locker room, following the trail of the thread, gathering it up as I walked, like Theseus in the labyrinth.

I must look awfully stupid, I thought. The one piece of luck I'd had so far today was that there was no one in the hall to see me.

I'd just reached the door to the gym when I heard footsteps on the stairs. Boy, that was fast, I thought. Bess must have run all the way.

"Thank goodness you're back," I said. "Two seconds more and I'd have been half-naked."

But it wasn't Bess.

"Then I'm sorry I didn't wait two seconds."

It was Steve Landis. Nice, smart, very attractive Steve Landis. For whom I'd harbored a secret longing for almost three months. Whom, at any other time, I would have been overjoyed to run into in an empty hallway.

I shrank back against the wall, clutched my books to my chest, and tried not to cry. But my misery must have shown on my face.

"Is something wrong, Nikki?" He came toward me. "You look like you're trying to hide from someone."

"No, no." My voice was shrill and unnatural. "Everything's fine."

Everything's just dandy. I finally get to be alone with Steve Landis, and my hair is wet and my sweater is coming apart and I have grape jelly on my jeans and I sound hysterical.

"Take advantage of the many wonderful opportunities that come your way!"

How? I can't move from this spot, he's thinking of me half-naked, and my voice has all the appeal of a chain saw.

At which moment Bess came running down the stairs yelling, "Nikki, I can't get your locker door open," and someone shoved the door of the gym out. It smashed into my back, sending me sprawling facedown on the floor.

"Nikki!" Three voices blended into one cry, and I groaned in pain.

I turned my head to the side. My eyes felt as if they were spinning in their sockets. Three sets of knees appeared in my line of vision. I was pretty dazed. I wasn't sure if there were really three people squatting next to me, or one person with six legs.

"I think I'm seeing triple," I whispered.

"Oh, Nikki, I'm sorry." Ms. Carlton's voice. "I didn't realize . . ."

Three pairs of hands reached down to help me to my feet. (Or one person with six arms, if I was seeing triple.)

"You poor kid," Steve said as I tried to steady myself on my feet. "Do you think anything's broken?"

"Only my faith in Stella Amarillo."

"Oh, dear," said Ms. Carlton. "She might have a concussion. We'd better get her to the nurse."

"Lean on me," Steve said. "I'll help you." He and Bess each put an arm around my waist and steered me toward the stairs.

My head clanged like a gong and my knees buckled as I walked.

"My thread," I told Bess. "I have to get the rest of my thread."

"Geez," said Steve sympathetically, "she must be delirious. And look at her sweater. It's completely wrecked."

* * *

"You're having a rough week," said the nurse as I lay on the same cot where I had recovered from meat loaf poisoning two days before.

I had an ice pad behind my head, an ice pack on my forehead, and was holding two ice cubes wrapped in a washcloth against my nose.

A scratchy wool blanket covered the rest of me, up to my chin. It felt itchy, even over my clothes, but all that ice was making me so cold that my teeth chattered. Which made my head hurt.

Every fifteen minutes the nurse peered into my eyes with a little flashlight, looking for signs of concussion.

And to make things absolutely perfect, Duane Bellinger lay on the cot next to me, separated only by a thin curtain, sneezing, coughing, and complaining that he had malaria.

In between sneezes, coughs, and moans, he begged my forgiveness for the jelly sandwich incident, and for my hand in marriage, if we both recovered.

When the nurse checked my eyes for the third time, I was feeling a little better. I pulled off the ice packs and began to worry about being in such close contact with Duane.

"Is malaria catching?" I asked her.

"He hasn't got malaria." She smiled. "Just allergies."

"The way my luck is running, I'll catch his allergies."

"Can I come in?" Steve Landis poked his head through the office door. "How's she doing?"

"I think she's going to be fine," the nurse said. "I want to get her X-rayed, but I can't reach her folks at work. I'll keep trying."

He moved close to my cot and looked down at me. At my swollen nose, my tangled hair, the egg-shaped lump on my forehead, which by now was probably an unbecoming shade of blue.

"Gee, you look awful."

"I know."

"Is there anything I can do for you?"

Just stop looking at me, I wanted to say. Just go away and come back when the bruises fade and my hair is brushed, and I'm wearing clothes that don't look like I stole them from a bag lady.

"Steve? Steve Landis, is that you?" Duane called from behind the curtain.

"Duane?" Steve pushed the curtain aside. "What's the matter? Your allergies again?"

"I think it's malaria. Did Nikki tell you we're engaged?"

"We're not engaged, Duane!" I sat up and swung my legs over the edge of the cot. "I'm getting out of here." I felt the air on my back as my sweater parted down the middle.

Would this day ever be over? Was there no end to the humiliation that I had to endure?

"There is something you can do for me," I told Steve. "If you could get my jacket from my locker, I'd really apprec — "

A sharp series of bells interrupted me.

"Fire drill," Steve said.

The nurse shook her head. "There's no fire drill scheduled for today."

"Attention please!" The principal's voice boomed over the PA system. "This is not a drill. It is imperative that we evacuate the building immediately. Your teachers will lead you in a calm and orderly manner to the nearest exit. I repeat, this is *not* a drill."

"Okay, kids, let's go," the nurse said.

"I can't go out like this," I said. "Let me get my jacket."

"It's probably just a bomb threat," Steve said.

"That's right," I agreed. "We have them a couple of times every year and there's never any bomb. Please don't make me go out like this."

Duane leaped to his feet and grabbed my arm. "I'll save you, Nikki." He yanked me up from my cot and sneezed on me.

"Take the blanket with you and let's go," the nurse ordered. "Duane, get moving."

"I'll help her." Steve draped the blanket over my shoulders. I clutched the edges together under my chin. He put his arm around me and guided me out of the office, into the stream of students surging down the hall.

Here was the moment I'd dreamed of for three months. Steve Landis, with his arm around me.

And bomb threat or no bomb threat, people noticed us.

"Hey, look!" yelled Robby Randazzo. "Sitting Bull."

"It can't be Sitting Bull," someone else said. "She's standing. Maybe it's Mother Teresa."

"No, Gandhi!" Shelby said as she passed us. "Nikki looks like Gandhi."

I lowered my head and fixed my eyes on the floor as Steve led me, in a calm and orderly manner, out of the building.

As we massed in the schoolyard, with my

classmates more concerned with my hideous appearance than the possibility of the school blowing up, I answered the question I'd asked myself before.

No. This day would never be over. And no. There was no end to the humiliation I would have to endure.

But the day did end.

And the school didn't blow up. The nurse was able to reach my father, and the X rays were negative. I didn't even have a concussion.

That night I reread my horoscope.

"Thursday, November 12: A red-letter day! All the signs are in your favor! Take advantage of the many wonderful opportunities that come your way!"

Snarling like a dog, I crumpled my horoscope into a ball and hurled it across the room. It landed in my tropical fish tank.

"Nikki, honey, are you all right?" my mother called. "Do you need anything?"

"Not unless you know a good exorcist!"

I started toward the aquarium to check my fish for injuries when the phone rang.

"Hey, Nikki, it's Steve. How's your head?"

"Steve?" I sat down on the edge of my bed

and clutched the phone to my ear. "Steve Landis?"

"Why are you so surprised?"

"Well — I didn't expect you to call." *Ever.*

"I feel sort of responsible for what happened," he said. "If I hadn't surprised you like that — "

"It's not your fault," I said. "It's my sweater's fault."

"How did the X rays turn out?"

"Fine," I said. I told myself he was just being nice because he felt guilty. I told myself he was just being nice because he was a basically nice guy. I told myself that anyone who'd seen what I'd been through today would be concerned.

There's no reason, I warned myself, to read more into Steve's call than simple courtesy.

I would be courteous, too. "I should have called to thank you," I said. "You went to a lot of trouble for me today."

"It wasn't any trouble," he said. "Do things like this happen to you a lot?"

I couldn't help laughing. "Only on my good days."

I explained to him about the horoscope, and then went on to describe everything that had gone wrong, up to the time Ms. Carlton slammed the gym door into me.

By the time I finished we were both laughing, and I realized we'd been on the phone for almost half an hour. This is more than simple courtesy, I thought. He could have hung up after I told him I was fine.

"Well," he said, "maybe you got all your bad luck a day early. And nothing will happen to you tomorrow."

"Tomorrow? Why should anything happen to me tomorrow?"

"Nikki, you're following your horoscope and you don't know what day tomorrow is?"

"It's Friday," I said, still puzzled. And then it hit me.

"Friday the thirteenth!" We both shouted it into the phone at the same time. We both groaned at the same time.

"It can't be any worse than today," I said when we finished groaning.

"Maybe I'd better keep an eye on you tomorrow, just in case," he said.

"Keep an eye on me?" When I had my hair brushed and decent clothes on and wasn't seeing triple?

"Can I pick you up in the morning?" he went

on. "I'm a very careful driver. Never had an accident."

I heard a thumping sound. "That's me, knocking on wood," he explained.

I was speechless. Steve Landis wanted to keep an eye on me. Steve Landis wanted to drive me to school. I could hardly breathe, let alone answer him.

"Nikki? Are you still there?"

I gulped. "Yes. Could you hold on a minute, please?"

I walked slowly to the fish tank and pulled the soggy horoscope from it. I squeezed out as much water as I could and carefully uncrumpled it.

I could just make out the forecast. "Friday, November 13: You may find this Friday the 13th living up to its reputation. Unlike yesterday, aspects are rather unfavorable. Postpone signing contracts or making long-term financial commitments. Above all, avoid joint partnership ventures."

I smiled happily and went back to the phone.

"Nikki, what are you doing?"

"Just checking my horoscope," I said.

"What did it say?" he asked.

"It said I should absolutely not let you drive me to school tomorrow."

He laughed. "It didn't really say that, did it?"

"Absolutely," I giggled.

For a moment he was silent. Then he said, "Okay. So should I pick you up around 7:45?"

I smiled into the phone even though he couldn't see me.

"Absolutely," I said.

ABOUT THE AUTHOR

Ellen Conford is a well-known young adult novelist whose books have earned her numerous awards, among them an IRA–CBC Children's Choice Award, an SLJ Best Book Award, and the 1983 California Young Reader Medal.

Some of the author's most popular books include *Dear Lovey Hart, I Am Desperate*, *A Royal Pain*, *We Interrupt This Semester for an Important Bulletin*, and *If This Is Love, I'll Take Spaghetti*, another collection of short stories.

Ms. Conford lives in Great Neck, New York.

point®

Other books you will enjoy, about real kids like you!